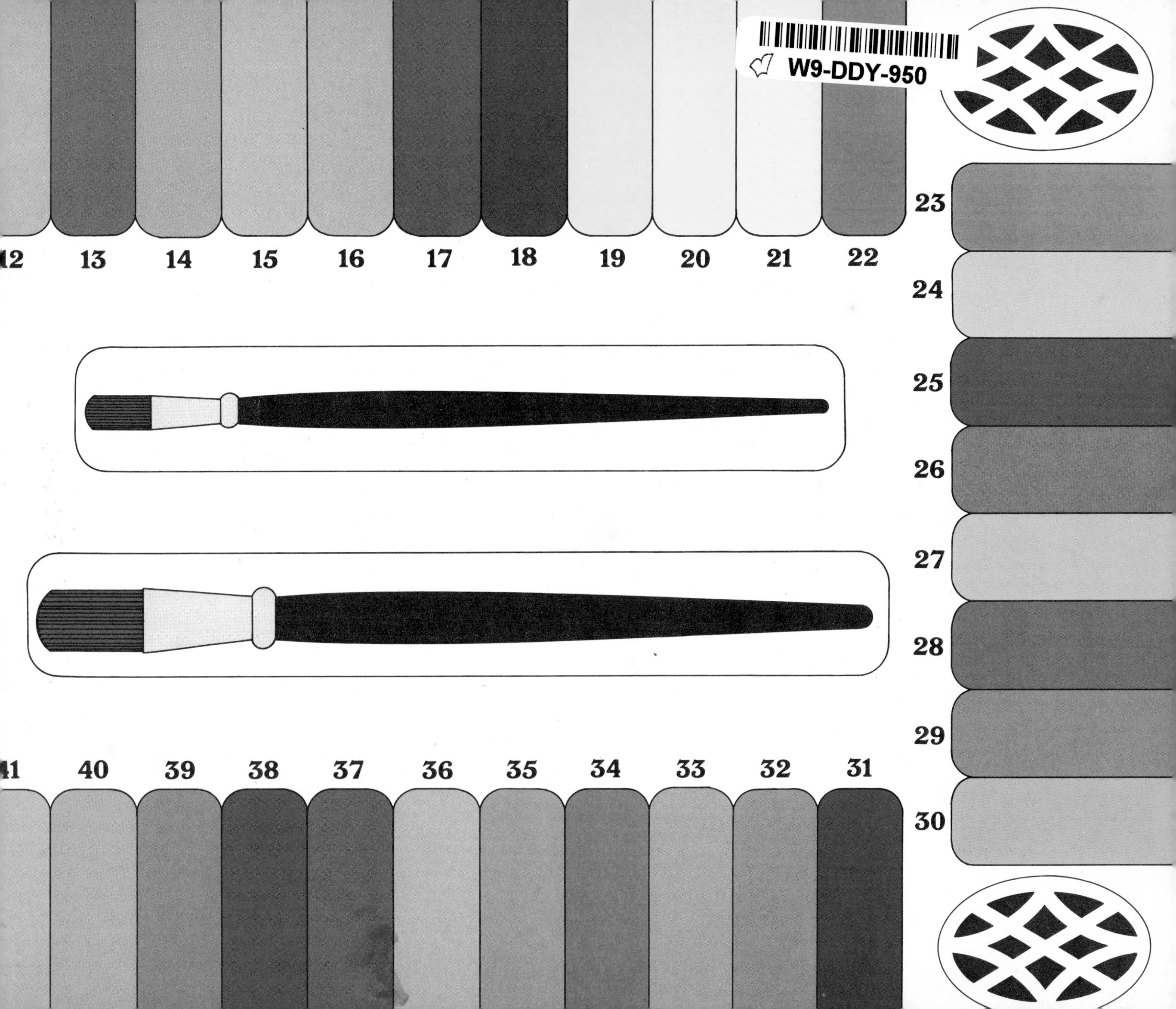
12
13
14
15
16
17
18
19
20
21
22
23
24
25
26
27
28
29
30
31
32
33
34
35
36
37
38
39
40
41

DECORATIVE PAINTING

Marg Pond

CHL CREATIVE HOME LIBRARY®
In Association with Better Homes and Gardens®
Meredith Corporation

ABOUT THE AUTHOR

Some thirty years ago, Marg Pond, midwestern housewife, mother, and now grandmother, discovered within herself an intense desire to create beautiful hand-painted flowers, fruits, figures, and designs to decorate her household items. She studied the few decorative painting books available and took a number of individual lessons. In the end, she found many of the painting procedures that she learned incomplete and difficult to follow. Considering herself representative of that group of persons with limited artistic talent, she vowed to record her painting methods step by step so that others interested in the subject would not experience the same frustrations she had.

Marg Pond kept her vow and has now taught thousands of individuals—both men and women here and abroad—her simple "no-talent" methods of achieving self-expression through decorative painting.

Library of Congress Cataloging in Publication Data

Pond, Marg, 1913-
Decorative painting.

1. Painting—Technique. 2. Art, Amateur.
I. Better homes and gardens. II. Title.
ND1473.P66 745.7'2 73-21913
ISBN 0-696-18950-X

Printed in the United States of America

CONTENTS

PREFACE

Learning the modern-day art of decorative painting can be one of the most exciting and rewarding experiences of your life. We are all born with a deep-seated need to create things of beauty, to interpret and reproduce in permanent form the fragile bits of nature that capture our eye. When man first walked upon the earth, every moment of his life was a struggle for survival. Yet he found time to beautify the walls of his cave, using soot from his torch and mineral-stained clay to paint his own image and that of the animals he hunted.

Each generation that followed found a method of applying color to its homes and to the things it used in everyday tasks. These were not people of great talent or skilled artisans who created things of value for kings and rulers. They were common folk—housewives and spinsters, farmers and soldiers—who found colors and designs to brighten the drabness of their possessions. Their "folk art" is treasured by their descendents and avidly sought by museums and private collectors.

A lasting form of folk art must be simple enough to be mastered by people who have no apparent "talent." It borrows from the best of the past and adds new concepts, techniques, and materials. It must be just difficult enough to present a challenge yet easy enough to be fun. The qualities of a successful folk artist seem to be a love of color, a strong desire to create, and a willingness to spend a sufficient amount of time in practice to master the simple techniques of the art.

The type of decorative painting you are about to begin is most enjoyable; students agree unanimously in that respect. It is based heavily on traditional design concepts, yet it offers much that is new. It can be learned easily by a sincere student. But is it an important art form? Will it last? After viewing an exhibit of student and staff projects, an outstanding artist, critic, teacher, and chairman of the fine arts department of a large state university was moved to predict: "I believe this may very well become known as the twentieth-century American folk art."

Regardless of what patterns you use or instructions you are given, something of *you* will be reflected in your decoration. Your own choice of colors and your renditions of designs will be distinct from any other—a portrayal of your creativeness and desire for self-expression. It is so exciting to watch a colorful design grow from your own fingers that you will become completely separated from everyday problems. You will spend a bit of time "in another world"—one that leaves you refreshed, relaxed, and a more interesting person.

MATERIALS

Tube colors: In theory, you could mix all the colors you will use with only five tubes of paint: red, yellow, blue, white, and black. In actual practice, it isn't quite that easy, and you could spend a great deal of time trying to arrive at the exact shade you want. To minimize mixing-and-matching time and to use this book with best results, you will need thirteen standard-sized tubes of oil paints. Since each oil-paint manufacturer describes its color differently, we had to choose one manufacturer's descriptive names to list. We chose Grumbacher because its line seems to be most widely available. If your art-supply store does not carry Grumbacher paints, simply tell your dealer what color you wish and he will translate it to a corresponding color in another line. The colors you will need are:

- Cadmium red light
- Grumbacher red
- Alizaran crimson
- Cadmium yellow medium
- Permanent green light
- Viridian green
- Prussian blue
- Cobalt violet
- Raw umber
- Burnt umber
- Burnt sienna
- Titanium white
- Ivory black

These pigments should not be mixed with other types of paints. Thin them with turpentine or with a few drops of cobalt dryer.

Make sure to squeeze tube colors from the bottom to prevent the formation of air pockets, which will dry out the paint remaining in the tube. Keep caps clean to prevent their sticking to the tube. If a cap should stick, hold a lighted match on it for a few seconds and then loosen. Unused tube colors can be lifted from the palette with your painting spatula and saved in an airtight fold-up package of waxed paper.

Cobalt dryer: A few drops of cobalt dryer are added to slower-drying oil colors to hasten the drying time. This is a particularly advisable practice when you are painting at high altitudes or in damp and humid areas. You will have to experiment to find the amount you need, beginning by adding two or three drops to the oil color. Your particular area may require as many as six drops.

The amount of paint you are using will also influence the amount of dryer necessary. Drying time of paint will vary from about three hours to overnight. If drying time is slower than this, add a few more drops the next time you paint.

One note of caution: Adding too much dryer will cause the paint to dry too quickly, leaving it dry on top and moist underneath. This will cause the paint to crack and peel from the decorated object.

Copal painting medium: Add copal painting medium by drops to thin slightly the tube colors. It is quite useful in keeping your paints of an even consistency for a longer period of time. Keep an eyedropper handy to dispense it, or just dip a clean spatula into the bottle, letting the mixture slide from the spatula tip by drops into the paint.

Kneaded eraser: Use a kneaded eraser much as you would a wallpaper cleaner, working it in your fingers until it is softened. It will hold the point or shape you desire. Use it to erase graphite tracing lines on your decorated objects or to erase other pencil marks.

Tracing paper and white typing paper: Use half a sheet of tracing paper at a time for practice lessons. Lay the sheet on top of the pattern, trace it with very light pencil, back it with a piece of white typing paper, clip it to your clipboard, and begin painting. For rough practice work on basic strokes or color testing, waxed paper can be used in the same way. Some types of coated (but not too slick) shelf paper also make excellent practice paper.

Shading sponge: Use a shading sponge to blend colors and to give texture to a design. Either buy a flat "elephant ear" sponge at any art supply store or make your own by cutting one-inch squares from foam-rubber pillow or chair padding.

Swatch chart: The numbered boxes going around the inside front cover of this book will be used to help you mix and match the oil colors in each lesson. You will rarely be able to match a color swatch *exactly* to your paints, so use the chart only as an approximate guide. Do not spend an undue amount of time trying to make a perfect match. When you have mixed a color similar to its corresponding swatch, consider it matched and proceed.

The swatch chart is also helpful in planning the colors of a composition because it lets you visualize the effect before mixing the colors.

Brushes and brush care: You need four brushes made of high-quality red sable:

- Large flat brush #7 or #8
- Small flat brush #4 or #5
- Large pointed brush #5 or #6
- Small pointed brush #1 or #2

The better grades of sable-tail hairs have the snap and resiliency that decorative painting requires. Inexpensive brushes, such as those made of the cheaper grades of red sable, fitch, sabeline, camel's hair, or bristles, are not suitable. These brushes will not hold their shape and will not deposit paint smoothly.

A good brush can be ruined very quickly, but given loving care, it will turn out good work for a long period of time. Memorize these points of brush care:

- Do not put aside a brush full of paint even for a few minutes. Take a few seconds to wash the brush in turpentine if you are interrupted while painting. Even a little paint remaining in the hairs next to the metal ferrule can cause the brush to lose its shape and make stray hairs stick out, which will cause ragged edges on your design.
- Never let your brushes rest on the hairs. Put them in a jar with the handles down, hairs up. Do not let them stand in turpentine for even a few seconds.
- When painting or when cleaning brushes, do not scrub. This will break the hairs. Stroke back and forth, lifting the tip at the end of a stroke.
- When you have finished painting, wash the brush several times in clear turpentine and then wash in lukewarm water and mild face soap. This is done by stroking the brush over the cake of soap several times and then stroking it in the palm of your hand. Repeat until no paint shows in the lather. Then rinse thoroughly. Reshape pointed brushes by rolling them between the thumb and forefinger. Reshape flat brushes to a chisel edge with the sides bowed in slightly at the tip.
- When you are storing your brushes between painting sessions, one further step will make your brushes last longer. Place a small dab of petroleum jelly in the palm of your hand and stroke the brush through it several times. Then reshape with your fingertips. Wash out in turpentine when you are ready to paint again.

When the flat brushes have finally given their all, the hairs will form a bushy bulge. The brush tips will separate and cause the fruit and flower edges to be fuzzy. But do not throw them away. They can later be used to streak and dry-brush additional colors over stained or antiqued surfaces to achieve an irregular effect (such as stippling) or even to poke stain or antiquing colors into the narrow areas of corners, carvings, and moldings.

Painting patterns: To use the pattern in each lesson, first trace it with light pencil onto tracing paper. Then back the tracing paper with regular white typing paper and clip both to your clipboard to paint. When painting on patterns that will be covered by an undercoat, trace the pattern design heavily enough so that it shows through.

Graphite paper: When you are ready to transfer a pattern to an object for decorating, use graphite paper—which can be found at any art-supply store—and follow these steps:

- Use either pencil or pen and ink to trace the pattern onto the tracing paper. If the pattern is larger than the sheet of tracing paper, tape together one or more pieces.
- Center the traced design on the object and secure at each side with small pieces of sticky tape.
- Find the coated side of the graphite paper and place it against the painted or stained surface as you continue to slide the graphite paper under the entire traced design.
- Use either an empty ballpoint pen or the sharp end of your small pointed brush to trace and transfer the design to the item. Use a very light pressure when tracing the design. The outline should be as faint as possible so that even a light color will cover it. There is no need to trace all details of a pattern. Stems, leaf veins, curliques, and other small details can be painted easily by your looking at the original pattern as you paint. Curliques should never be traced. They are more graceful when painted freehand.
- Later, when the paint is dry, any remaining graphite lines may be easily removed with the kneaded eraser or the corner of a cloth dampened with soap and water or a bit of turpentine.
- The graphite lines will show clearly on all painted or stained surfaces except on black or very dark colors. If you want to trace onto an object that has a dark background, pick up some dressmaker's carbon at your local dime or fabric store.

Graphite paper can be used to transfer a design to plastic items, all papers, shade cloth, white milkglass, or white china. Clear glass is the only surface to which tracing will not adhere. If you use clear glass, you will have to decorate it freehand. This is no problem because you will soon learn to paint flowers and designs without having to trace them.

Clear glass is more attractive when it has a little background color. This can be accomplished in one of several ways:

- Fill the clear glass containers with something both useful and colorful, such as colored cotton balls or tiny bars of colored soap.
- Use a colored spray paint to add either a faint haze of color or a definite spatter effect. To create a transparent haze of color, stand back three or four feet and quickly wave the spray over the glass. Repeat this until enough color is added for a pleasing effect. A spatter of color can be achieved by moving closer to the glass container and pressing the nozzle quickly on and off in a series of short sprays. Paint and/or hardware stores stock many colors of spray-type paints, in both flat and gloss finishes.
- If you choose, the entire glass object can be covered with a colored paint and decorated when it is dry. Again, your paint or hardware dealer will be helpful in advising you about various kinds of spray or brush-on paints.

Miscellaneous materials: You'll need a hard, smooth work surface, such as a clipboard, or a piece of lightweight wood about 8 by 10 inches will do. If it's of soft wood, you can hold your work with thumb tacks or pushpins. Use sticky tape if you choose pressed board or hard wood.

Purchase a can of spray fixative at an art-supply store. This is a clear acrylic spray that comes in either a gloss or matte finish. It is usually used as a protective film for charcoal and pastel drawings, but you will use it to hasten the drying time of wet oil colors.

Use either a disposable palette pad or a glass window pane for mixing your paints. The first may be purchased at an art-supply store and the latter at a hardware store.

Later you will need a crow quill pen and waterproof black ink with which to do detail. These are available at office-supply and stationery stores.

You will need a supply of turpentine for cleaning your brushes and thinning your paint. Pure gum spirits of turpentine are available in cans at any paint or hardware store. Do *not* use any other solvents, such as alcohol, gasoline, lighter fluid, the so-called universal solvents, or mixtures containing carbon tetrachloride.

An empty fruit jar will come in handy for storing dirty turpentine until it can be poured into the ground in a spot where it won't harm vegetation. Never pour turpentine into your sewage system! Save the turpentine, if you wish, and let the paint settle to the bottom. You can use it in some of the antiquing mixes described later in book.

You will also need a supply of tissue—napkins, facial, or toilet—some soft rags, a bit of terry cloth, a heavy jar or pot to hold your brushes, and a small juice or vegetable can to hold the turpentine you are using while painting.

Save your large grocery sacks and use them as disposable waste baskets.

A roll of waxed paper or slightly glazed shelf paper will be very useful if kept close at hand.

Purchase a painting spatula from either an art-supply store or the hardware department. You will use the spatula for a variety of tools—from gauging the thinness of your paint and mixing colors to cleaning your palette of unused colors for future work.

Save your clothing by wearing a smock or an old shirt when you paint, and save your manicure by working moist face soap in around your fingernails before you start. After painting, use a waterless hand cleaner to remove any dried paint on hands or clothing.

Getting organized: The first thing to organize is your time. Try to plan how much time each day or week you will devote to painting. The lessons in this book are planned to average one lesson per week, but some readers may need a little more time and some a little less. If you have more time available and are serious about becoming a good decorative artist, paint each of the lesson assignments. How *quickly* you complete the book is of no importance. How *well* you paint is your primary concern.

Do not skip around, but paint the lessons in order. You will, no doubt, have favorite subjects and will want to skip over lessons that have less appeal to you. But, skipping lightly over less-favored lessons will leave you unable to paint other later compositions. Each lesson builds upon itself, gradually adding and combining certain skills and techniques. Many good reasons may arise to prevent you from doing a lesson every week. When this happens, make sure to review the past lessons when you again resume your painting sessions. Do not become rusty between lessons and lose, because of lack of practice, the skills you have developed.

Choose a pleasant and comfortable work area. A card table is about the right height and is large enough to hold your tools. Almost any armless, straight-backed chair will be fine if it seats you at a comfortable level. A natural light coming over your left shoulder is ideal. Try to choose a spot where you can leave your work table between painting sessions, without having to pack up everything and put it away—you may find some unexpected extra moments when you can sit down and dash off a painting.

The following list describes the best tool arrangement for a right-handed person.

- Tube colors, with labels up, on the left side.
- Jar of brushes in the center.
- Palette to the right.
- Open can of turpentine behind the palette.
- To the right of the palette, spatula resting on a stack of tissue so that you can wipe it off after each use and drop the tissue straight down into the grocery sack-waste basket.
- A large rag on your lap.

LESSON 1

Basic Strokes; Simple Flowers and Leaves

In this introduction, you will learn how to mix paints; how to fill your brushes to paint two-toned, shaded strokes; and how to paint the basic brush strokes using both the flat and the pointed brushes. At the conclusion of Lesson 1, you will use several of the basic brush strokes to paint the imaginative flower and leaves in Photograph #4.

Before putting any paint on your palette, read the complete text and step-by-step directions for each lesson. Almost any problem can be solved by simply reading the lesson again or by holding a few extra painting sessions. You'll find that learning to paint is quite simple and can be easily mastered from the very beginning of the course.

Painting can truly be called a therapy. It relaxes, refreshes, and renews our enthusiasm for life. Two or three hours of painting time will race by as quickly as thirty minutes and you will end the session feeling fulfilled and satisfied.

Mixing Paints

Before you begin to mix the shades of paint for each lesson, be sure to stack several layers of inexpensive, disposable tissue near the right side of your palette and to have a spatula nearby. If you are left-handed, keep the tissue and spatula on the left side of the palette. You will find the stack of tissue a real help in providing a throw-away cleaning rag for your paint-filled brushes or spatula.

Place the oil colors on the upper left side of your palette and titanium white on the upper right area. In this way you will have freed the entire center area of your palette for mixing your shades of paint. Be sure to leave at least two or three inches of space between the edges of each pool of color so that you'll have room to stroke around the edges without brushing into another pool.

After stroking around the edges of each pool, use the spatula to clean up the brush strokes. Wipe the spatula in the sheets of tissue and dispose of them in a large paper bag. Spatula cleaning around the paint pools is essential since stroking over a used area will only dilute the color on your brush or cause the brush to pick up another color.

Obtaining the Right Paint Consistency

As a beginning artist, your first basic-stroke exercises should be executed with a thin paint, just thin enough to drip slowly from the spatula. This is also the consistency to use for painting borders, scrollwork, stems, and ribbons.

If the paint stands in rounded mounds or thick ridges, add a few drops of copal painting medium and a drop or two of turpentine to thin it. The paint will also grow a little thicker as it lies on the palette and is exposed to moving air. Adding a few drops of the copal painting medium will help keep the paint moist and of an even consistency for a longer period of time.

When the brush begins to skip or you have lost the shaded effect, wipe the brush or squeeze it out in your lap rag and fill it again. Don't, however, fill the brush in the same spot of paint and don't fill the same side of the brush you used before. Move a little farther around the pool so that you have a clean patch for the dry side of your brush.

Watch your palette when you add the second shading color. Begin to paint only when the colors merge and blend together.

Later on, with practice, you'll know by the look and feel of the brush stroke when the paint is of the right consistency to produce an easily flowing stroke. Remember to keep your paint just thin enough to flow easily yet still cover the background color. As you progress through the lessons, you'll learn how much pressure is needed for painting with slightly thicker paint.

Painting on waxed paper is ideal for practice sessions, but its waxed surface prevents you from producing your best finished work, particularly fruit. Tracing paper provides an easier painting surface for your lessons and will later serve as a quick guide to color selection for objects you will be decorating. Of course, the most valuable experience you can possibly have is to actually decorate a painted surface. Besides providing the most satisfaction, you'll learn more quickly the proper paint consistency needed for various surfaces.

Filling Your Brushes

Throughout the first few lessons, the typical beginner tends to be a little fearful of the brush. Don't be! These brushes are your decorating tools, and they are just waiting to be put to work. They may look delicate, but they're capable of withstanding the firm pressure needed for them to be filled properly.

How to fill a brush with paint is not at all difficult to learn. With a little practice, it will soon become so automatic that you won't give a second thought to filling the brush with two or even three colors for shaded strokes. Here's how to do it:

Pointed brushes: The movement used to fill the brushes can be compared to the back-and-forth swing of a clock pendulum—swing the brush across the outside edge of the paint, and lift it slightly at the end of each swinging stroke so that the hairs are in straight alignment and ready for the next filling stroke. Do not stick the brush into the center of the pools of color, but rather into the outside edges.

Many beginning painters are a bit timid about exerting enough pressure to fill properly the large pointed brush. Use enough pressure to force the long hairs of the brush into a fan shape as it is stroked into

Photograph #4

the edge of paint. The silver ferrule should be pressed against the palette as you stroke. This allows the sable hairs to absorb and hold the paint along the entire length of the brush.

There is a very simple trick to filling the pointed brush with two colors. Each time you stroke back and forth into the edge of the pool of paint, slide the brush in a little deeper. Experiment a little, and you will probably discover that it takes about ten or twelve strokes—each one creeping a little deeper into the paint—to fill about three-fourths of the brush. Then, turn the unfilled side of the brush toward the contrasting color and creep into the pool just as before. You'll probably need only four or five strokes to finish filling it.

The most important thing to remember about filling the brush is to confine the back-and-forth strokes to an inch or so in length. If your filling strokes are longer than this, you will be painting only a longer swath of color on your palette instead of working the paint up into the brush. The unfilled portion of the brush will always be on a dry portion of the palette as the opposite side is being filled with the paint.

Whenever you refill your brushes with color, do not stroke in the same spot you have used before. Move to another side of the pool of color so that you have a clean area for the dry side of the brush.

Carefully watch the brush as it fills with paint and becomes more fanlike with each stroke. The more paint you can work up into the hairs, the longer you will be able to paint before refilling. Remember to flatten the brush into a fan shape as you fill it.

Whenever you want a leaf or flower to appear equally shaded with light and dark color, fill the brush about three-fourths full of the lighter color and then add fewer strokes of the deeper color to the opposite side of the brush. This suggestion is helpful in filling either the pointed or the flat brush.

Flat brushes: The flat brushes are filled in the same manner as the pointed brushes, but since they are already flattened, you will not need to use as much pressure. They also hold less paint than the pointed brushes, so they require less stroking to fill them.

After filling about three-fourths of the brush with a lighter color, turn the unfilled portion of the brush into the edge of the deeper color and take fewer strokes to complete filling. When you have moved completely around the pool of color, clean the palette. Either scrape up the blended color around the edge of the pool with your spatula and wipe it off on your tissue, leaving a fresh, clean border around the pools, or just use the spatula to lift the paint to another spot, scraping up the entire used area all at once.

If you are tempted to dabble into the pool of paint, you will find that it is impossible to keep the colors separated in the brush or to produce a nicely shaded stroke. Remember to stroke straight back and forth, lifting the brush slightly at the end of the stroke so that you will not damage the hairs. With just a little practice, making two- and three-toned strokes will become a habit.

Preparation for Practice Lesson

To practice the basic strokes of this lesson, you will need to mix a red shade and a pink shade. For more variety in the future, you might experiment with other shades in the swatch chart whenever you are practicing the basic strokes. Just be sure that the contrast between the two shades is enough that they do not merge and become one color as they are painted.

Brushes

Pointed brush strokes (Pattern #1)	Large pointed brush
Flat brush strokes (Pattern #2)	Large and small flat brushes
Basic leaves (Pattern #3)	Large and small flat brushes
Lesson flower (Pattern #4)	Large pointed brush (or large flat brush if you would like to experiment)

Colors

Basic brush strokes and lesson flower

Red	Grumbacher red mixed with titanium white to match swatch #1.
Pink	Titanium white added to some of above shade to match swatch #3.

Basic leaves and lesson flower (do not mix until ready to paint)	
Darker green	Permanent green light mixed with a bit of burnt umber and titanium white (similar to swatch #17).
Lighter green	Titanium white added to some of above shade (similar to swatch #15).

Mixing Shades

Red shade: To mix red shade, spread Grumbacher red into the center area of your palette, using your spatula. Clean the spatula in tissue, then dip it into the bottle of copal painting medium, and add a few drops to the red paint. Add turpentine to thin the paint slightly when necessary. Mix the paint, the copal, and the turpentine by using the spatula to turn the paint over and to blend it. Clean the spatula in the tissue again, and spread some titanium white near the top right corner of your palette. Add the titanium white, bit by bit, to some of the red until you have mixed a shade similar to swatch #1. Add a few more drops of turpentine if necessary.

Pink shade: Pick up a little of the above shade on the tip of the spatula, and place it two or three inches away from the pool of red. Add white until you have mixed a shade similar to swatch #3. If all the white has been used on your palette, replace it with only as much as you can use within a short period of time.

Darker green: Place permanent green light on the lower part of the palette. Add a little titanium white, a bit at a time, and a bit of the burnt umber until you have an olive green shade similar to swatch #17.

Lighter green: Divide the above shade and add titanium white to one of the pools until you have a contrasting lighter green shade similar to but not matching swatch #15.

Pointed Brush Strokes

We'll start by painting the large commas on line a, Pointed Brush Strokes, Pattern #1. Have several pieces of waxed paper ready on which to practice.

Dip the large pointed brush in turpentine, and squeeze it dry. Stroke into the edge of the pink paint, pressing the brush firmly into a fan shape as you creep a little deeper into the paint with each back-and-forth filling stroke. When you have taken ten or twelve strokes, the brush will be about three-fourths full and will look flattened and slightly fanned out in shape.

Turn the unfilled side of the brush into the red paint and fill it just as before. You will need fewer filling strokes of the red (about five or six) to fill the brush completely. If you want the deeper shade of paint to predominate, take fewer filling strokes of the lighter shade and more filling strokes of the deeper shade. You can add fewer strokes of the deeper color because it will take over the lighter color as it is added.

Now you are ready to paint. Hold the brush in the same way that you hold a pen when you write. You may prefer to extend your little finger and let it steady

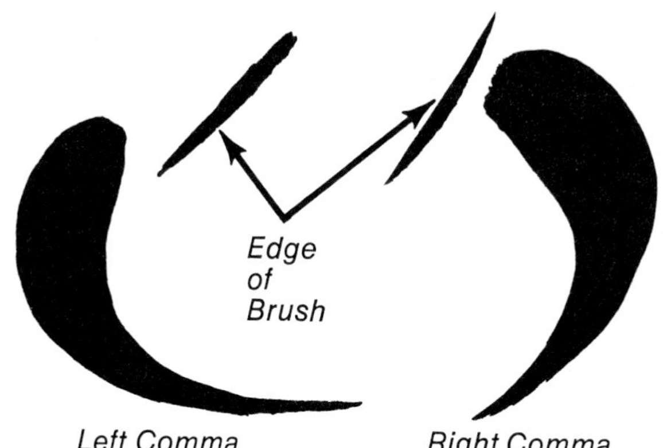

Pattern #1 Pointed Brush Strokes

your hand on the clipboard. You may feel more relaxed if you rest your forearm on the edge of the table, at least until you have found your most comfortable position. Be relaxed.

Begin these comma strokes to the right, and place the flattened tip ends of the pointed brush at a slight angle.

Use a very firm pressure as you lean back on the brush so that the metal ferrule lies firmly against the surface. Begin to move the brush slowly into a large curved comma. As you begin to move the brush, *gradually* lessen the pressure so that the metal ferrule is slowly lifted and only the tip of the brush remains against the surface to form a fine, tapered line.

Do not hurry to end this stroke—you'll only paint an abrupt, stubby ending if you quickly jerk the brush to end the stroke. *You must paint these slowly and deliberately.* The finished effect is always perfect if your brush is properly filled to capacity, the paint is of thin consistency, and the pressure is firm to begin with and light at the end of each stroke. All the basic strokes take only about three or four seconds to complete, so there's no need to hurry.

Now relax and paint more of them—very large ones, filling the whole page. Try curving the comma into a large C or a big U, painting from right to left. Don't worry about painting these strokes as small as those shown in the pattern. It is easier to learn the various brush pressures by painting large before painting small.

Never work in a cramped position. Shift the clipboard or turn it upside down to give yourself an easy working angle. This is true for decorating any object.

Now try painting the commas from left to right. If you are right-handed, painting from left to right may seem awkward for a while, but it will soon become easy with a little practice.

Now put a series of commas together and paint the border designs on lines b and d. The border design on line c is lots of fun. Make the wavy line by varying the pressure on the brush. Now see how easy it is to make a simple flower by using just the comma strokes shown on line e. You'll have to turn the board upside down, since you'll always start your stroke on the wide end of the comma. When finished, wash the brush out in turpentine.

Flat Brush Strokes

Now that you have seen the pointed brush at work and some of the things it can do, try your hand at the large flat brush. Most beginners find that flat brushes are easier to use and can create about the same effects as a pointed brush. Throughout these lessons, you will be using flat brushes most of the time, but don't put your pointed brush away and forget about it. It's very important for painting flowing ribbons, turned leaves, borders, and scrollwork. You will need to know how to handle both types.

If you have used all the pink and red paint, clean the palette and mix more of these colors for the flat brush strokes, Pattern #2. The strokes on line a are painted by pressing the flat brush down as wide as it will go and sliding the brush downward. The shorter strokes are formed by slightly pressing and lifting the brush. The press-strokes will be used later in many designs.

In line b, the brush is held perfectly straight and the flat end is lightly pressed straight down. This exercise is often used to create a stippled effect.

The c and d designs are both painted with the small flat brush. C is made by a series of lightly curved pivot strokes to form petals with a U shape.

The d design is formed by a series of short press-strokes. Both c and d will be used frequently to form small blossoms and flowers.

E and f are excellent exercises for learning to use the corners of the flat brush and to regulate brush pressure and lift for different effects.

G is painted with the entire brush held flat against the surface as your arm guides the brush into slight waves.

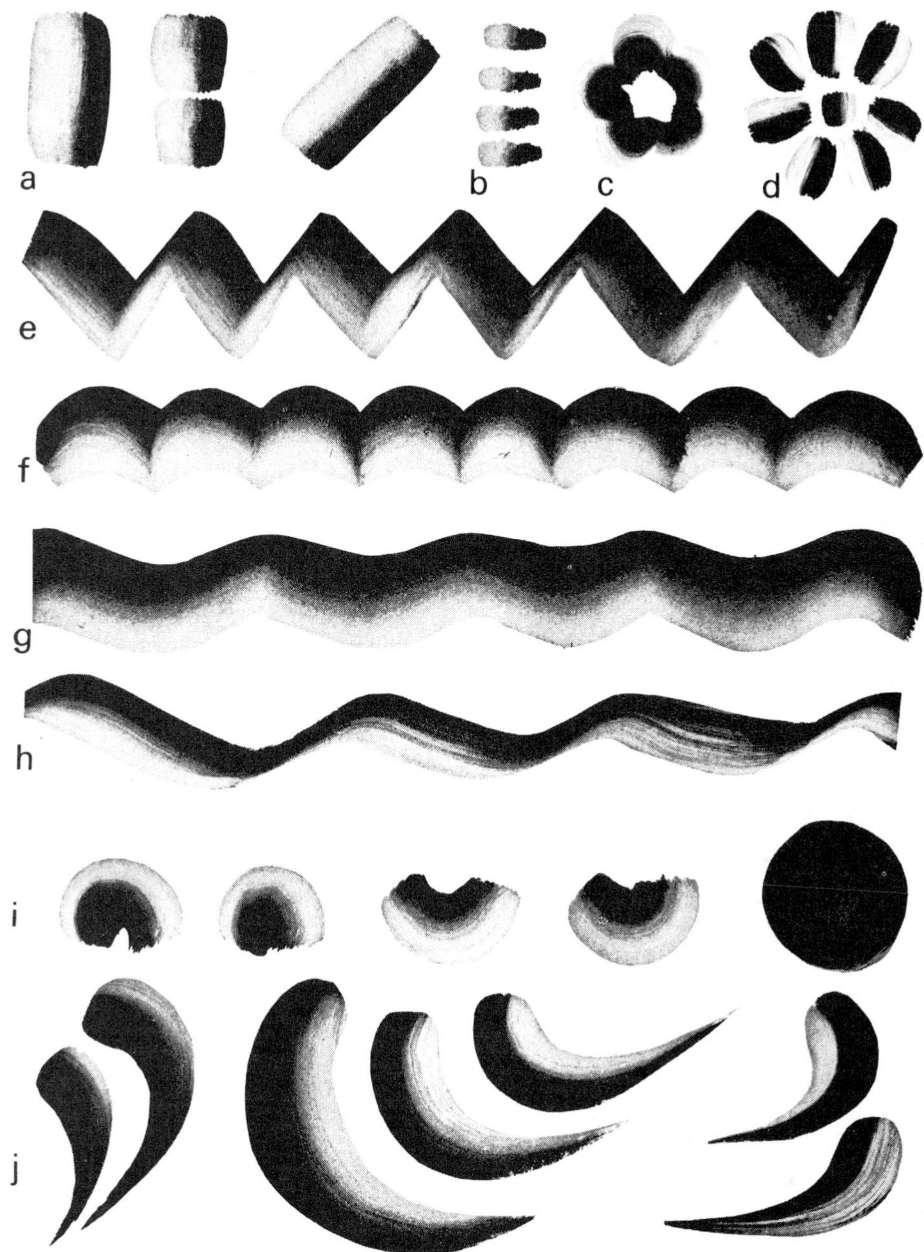

Pattern #2 Flat Brush Strokes

Pattern #3 Basic Leaf Strokes

You painted a ribbon with the pointed brush by changing the amount of pressure. Now you will paint a ribbon, h, by rolling the brush in your fingers about a quarter-turn and then returning to the original position. The wrist is held motionless while the arm and hand move across the paper.

The strokes in the i line provide the groundwork for the cherries and gooseberries that you will be painting later.

The comma strokes in line j are painted with the flat brush placed at the same slight angle used for the pointed brush strokes. Press firmly to start the stroke, and gradually lessen the pressure as the brush is slowly curved and lifted until only the corner of the brush remains against the surface to end the stroke with a fine tapered line. By tipping the flat brush to either corner, you will be able to paint a tapered ending exactly like that of the pointed brush stroke.

Beginners are generally timid about pressing the brush firmly to its widest capacity. Experiment a bit. See how large a stroke you can make with your brushes. Then try pressing very lightly to see how small a stroke you can make with the same brushes. You will be surprised at how small a stroke can be painted with a large brush and light pressure. Remember always to start your stroke at the large, or "fat," marks of the pattern, diminishing to a fine point.

These basic strokes are the foundation of decorative painting. How successful you are in the more advanced lessons will be determined by your ability to do these strokes well and to vary them for different types of design motifs. The more you practice the basic strokes, the easier your painting will become. Just as is true of penmanship, you cannot practice them too much. Every time you have a bit of paint left over, use it by doing a few of these strokes. Do not skip over some that you do not like as well as others. You will need to do them all well. Soon you will manage the brushes as easily as you do a pen. The practice necessary in beginning decorative painting can be compared to the practice necessary in learning any new skill. You must begin with a solid foundation of skills before you can progress.

Lesson Pattern

You are now ready to put several of the strokes together and paint the simple flower of Lesson #1. Cut a sheet of tracing paper in half, place it over Pattern #4, and copy the design. Place a sheet of white typing paper behind the tracing paper, and clip both sheets to your clipboard. Paint all the red-to-pink sections of the flower. While this is drying, mix some shades of green paint, following color instructions, and practice the basic leaf strokes (Pattern #3).

To do simple leaves, once again you'll mix two pools of color—a light green and a dark green—and blend them together in the leaf strokes. Fill the large flat brush with the two contrasting shades of green, as described in "Filling Your Brushes." Although these two shades contrast, they will blend together as the stroke is applied and will produce a light-to-dark shaded leaf. Below is an open illustration of a simple leaf, which is painted with only two brush strokes. The first is a comma stroke to form the short side of the leaf. The second is a trailing S to form the longer side of the leaf. The trailing S slightly overlaps the comma and wraps around it. Either the darker green shade can be applied to the outside edges of the leaf, or you can paint a leaf with light edges and a darker center.

Pattern #4

Right Comma

Left Comma

As soon as you have mastered the simple leaf, go back to Pattern #4 and add the stem and leaves to your design. When completed, wash out your brushes in turpentine.

This has been a long lesson. Very few beginners can finish it, and do the exercises well, in a two-hour session. Most of these basic strokes will be a part of the designs you will paint throughout a variety of lessons. Although it's interesting to be able to perfect them while you paint an attractive pattern, it's much more satisfying to have them under control before undertaking a design so that your progress will follow a steady progression.

These basic strokes are fundamental to decorative painting, and it's impossible to practice them too much. The shaded brush stroke is a technique to be learned only through constant practice; once learned, it is yours forever.

Simple flower and basic comma strokes decorate a metal windowbox. By Yee Chea Lin.

Photograph #5

LESSON 2

Blossom Types

The blossom and fill-in flower that you will learn to paint in this lesson will be used frequently throughout future flower and fruit designs. As in this lesson, blossoms can be used for an entire design. Or, by changing the color and size, they can become the small blossoms surrounding fruits, such as strawberries, peaches, plums, or cherries.

The fluffy little fill-in flower, which is one of the most versatile flowers, is used, as its name implies, to fill in areas needing something more than leaves. As in this pattern, it may also be used to extend the design gracefully in length or width. It can also be used to add another color to a design. This is done by painting the fill-in flower a contrasting color.

The curliques in this pattern are also used frequently in designs. They are often used with grape or strawberry designs and lend a graceful fill-in for nearly any flower composition.

To paint this lesson, use tracing paper to copy the design of Pattern #5, except for the curliques. Slip a piece of white typing paper beneath the tracing paper, and clip both sheets to your clipboard.

When you are ready to transfer a design to an item for decoration, follow the steps suggested under the head "Graphite Paper," page 8. In fact, when you have finished this lesson, why not paint its design on something right away? This will give you valuable experience in transferring a pattern: You will learn how to gauge the pressure when using the graphite paper, how thick the paint must be in order to cover the traced outline, and how various surfaces—metal, wood, and plastic—feel under your brush. In the future, have an article or two on hand to decorate using the lesson you have just painted. You will nearly always have mixed enough paint to decorate several items. And even as a beginner, your work will be far prettier than that on many items you will see for sale.

We will begin to paint this lesson by placing the green shade in the center of the palette. Use your spatula to place a little white nearby to use in shading the blossoms. Add a drop or two of copal painting medium or turpentine to thin the paint slightly if necessary. You will find that flowers can be painted with paint slightly thicker than that used in the first lesson. The thinner consistency used for the basic strokes will be necessary only when you are painting borders, scrollwork, or other long, flowing strokes.

Brushes

Blossoms and leaves	Large flat brush
Stems, leaf veins, curliques, and flower centers	Small pointed brush

Colors

Blossoms and fill-in flower	Viridian green mixed with titanium white to match swatch #11. Titanium white for shading.
Blossom centers	Cadmium yellow medium mixed with a bit of titanium white to match swatch #19.
Leaves (do not mix until ready to paint) Darker shade	Permanent green light mixed with a bit of cadmium yellow medium, a bit of raw umber, and enough titanium white to match swatch #37, thinned with copal painting medium if necessary.
Lighter shade	Titanium white added to some of the above shade to match swatch #39, thinned with copal painting medium if necessary.
Stems, leaf veins, curliques, and blossom center accents	A bit of burnt umber added to the above deeper green shade (similar to swatch #38), thinned with turpentine.

Pattern #5

Lesson Pattern

Blossoms

Mix the colors for blossoms, fill-in flowers, and blossom centers. Fill the entire flat brush with short filling strokes of the green-blue shade #37. When this is completed, stroke one side of the brush into the edge of the white. About two or three short filling strokes will be needed before a slight blending shows on the palette and an edge of white remains along the side of the brush.

Begin painting one of the large double-petal blossoms in the center of the design. Paint a short comma on the right half of the petal, keeping the white side of the brush on the outside edge of the petal. Then reverse the brush, turning the white side to the left, and paint the left side of the petal, slightly overlapping in the center. (You may need to pick up an edge of white to complete the opposite half of the petal.)

Refill the brush with the blue-green and white as necessary, and complete painting all the larger outside petals. Now, before the petals dry, use the white to paint the inside smaller petals. Some of the blue-green color should remain in the brush to help shade the smaller petals.

Now gently push the flat edges of the brush hairs into the white so that the white is picked up across only the tip of the brush. With light pressure, paint the inside petals with a short press-stroke (as in line a of the "Flat Brush Strokes," Pattern #2). Paint the blossoms from the outside into the center.

Another way to shade the smaller blossoms is to fill the brush lightly with the blue-green color and then add an edge of white to each side of the flat brush. Use the press-stroke to paint each shaded blossom.

When all the double blossoms and large single blossoms are painted, use the press-stroke to paint the remaining small blossoms.

Blossom Centers

Mix a small amount of the yellow shade, fill the small pointed brush with it, and paint a series of small dots in the center of the blossom. Clean the brush and add a few dots of white around the yellow centers. Later on, when you have painted the leaves and stems, come back to the blossoms and add a few accent dots to the centers with the darker shade of green.

Leaves and Stems

Use your spatula to lift aside any remaining flower colors. We will use them later to add the fill-in flower to the design.

After mixing the light and darker shades of green, you are ready to paint the shaded leaves according to the instructions in Lesson 1. The stems are painted with the deeper shade of green, which is thinned with drops of turpentine until it is very thin. Use just the tip of your small pointed brush to add the stems and thin twig effect of the fill-in flower. Remember to add a few accents of this color to the blossom centers.

Fill-in Flower

This flower is so simple to paint that it hardly needs explanation.

Simply fill one side and corner of your brush with the blue-green paint. Then tip the same corner lightly into the white so that both the blue-green and the white are on the same corner. Using the paint-filled corner of the brush, lightly dot or pat the colors on the design. Add both colors on the brush corner frequently because such a small amount of paint will be used quickly. Pat or dot the colors more heavily around the blossoms and add fewer dots near the stem endings. This flower should look very light and graceful—the easiest way to keep it this way is to paint only a light suggestion of a stem throughout the flower.

Curliques

These will look more graceful if you do not trace them onto the pattern. Just relax and paint them freehand. Use the darker shade of green you have mixed for the stems, keeping it very thin with turpentine. Hold the small pointed brush in a vertical position with the hand, wrist, and arm relaxed.

Pick up a little of the paint and try a few. Don't be discouraged if they aren't perfect. With practice, they will become easier and easier to do.

Lunch box trimmed with fill-in flowers and a comma stroke border. By Yee Chea Lin.

LESSON 3

General Instructions for Painting Fruit: Pears

Despite the differences in color and shape, each type of fruit is painted with the same basic techniques, using the same four steps: (1) undercoat; (2) deepen and shade; (3) dry-brush and blend; and (4) lighten and highlight. Study the following descriptions of each step before starting more advanced lessons on painting fruit.

1. *Undercoat:* This is the base color, which is usually applied in a single tone. Fruit, for example, is outlined and filled in with a single color, using a flat brush. The paint should flow easily and smoothly, leaving no high ridges or thick brush marks. If this occurs, add a few more drops of modifier or turpentine to thin the paint. The modifier will keep the paint moist for a longer period of time than the turpentine, which is only a temporary thinner and must be added more often.

The undercoat should be applied generously just inside the pattern outline. If necessary, apply the undercoat a second time to cover well. When painting the undercoat for fruit, always use a generous amount of paint because dry-brushing, sponging, and blending will remove some of it.

The brush is not to be cleaned in turpentine after the undercoating but is, instead, gently squeezed in tissue to remove the excess paint. The reason that the brush is not washed in turpentine is that a small amount of turpentine might remain in the brush and cause the wet undercoat to be removed as the deeper shade is applied in the next step.

2. *Deepen and shade:* This direction is most frequently given in the instructions for painting fruit, but it will also be used from time to time with other subject matter. The flat brush is used for this step.

To fill the brush with the deeper shading color, stroke about one-fourth of the brush into the edge of the paint, taking about two short filling strokes. As you apply the deeper shading color, extend it to the outline, smoothly catching in the undercoat along the outside edges. The outside edge and corner of the brush will be working for you in this process, smoothly blending the sides of the fruit as it paints.

Be sure the shading colors are just moist enough to flow easily when light pressure is applied to the brush. Then tip the brush to the outside as you add the color, so that the fruit edges are sharp and clear.

When adding the shading colors over the wet undercoat, wipe the brush frequently to remove any undercoat that has been picked up on the brush. Repeat this step to complete the outlining.

Deeper shading can be achieved either by using more dark paint in the brush or by taking extra strokes to darken some areas.

3. *Dry-brush and blend:* This term means to paint with the brush dry—thoroughly squeezed in tissue but not cleaned in turpentine. Dry-brushing is used to pull together two different shades for a blended effect of light and dark shading.

It is important always to dry-brush, blend, and shade with a light touch, wiping the brush frequently to remove excess paint. Curve the light, blending strokes to follow the contour of the fruit or other design. The brush should never be cleaned in turpentine until the fruit is entirely finished. Just wipe and squeeze it in tissue and a lap rag before adding another color. This is of special importance when adding the highlight. Cleaning the brush in turpentine before all shading is completed will cause the damp brush to remove the fruit colors that are underneath.

You may also use a sponge or small piece of cloth wrapped around your index finger to blend the colors together. Coarser sponges will give a more

Photograph #6

heavily textured effect, which you may prefer. When using the sponge or cloth to blend, use the same light touch, frequently turning to a fresh area. When you have completed the fruit, clean the sponge in turpentine and squeeze it dry with a lap rag.

4. *Lighten and highlight:* To lighten an area for contrast, lightly pat on an irregular patch of color with a brush. Then lightly sponge or dry-brush it to blend.

A highlight is a short stroke applied to the lightened area to suggest light reflecting off the object. The highlights are added when the fruit colors are still wet so that the effect is a blended one rather than one harshly contrasting.

Since the undercoat for fruit must remain moist until the shading is completed, most of the fruit lessons will be painted with straight oil colors, thinned slightly with a few drops of modifier or turpentine. These colors will be slow to dry, but this is an advantage when you are learning to shade and blend.

After you have learned this technique, you can hasten the drying time by adding a few drops of dryer or by using a spray fixative when you have finished.

Brushes

Pears and leaves	Large flat brush
Stems and detail	Small pointed brush

Colors

Upper Pear	
Undercoat	Cadmium yellow medium mixed with titanium white to match swatch #19, thinned with two or three drops of modifier.
Deepen and shade	Permanent green light mixed with burnt sienna, and titanium white if necessary (similar to swatch #17 or #38).
Lighten and highlight	Titanium white, thinned with modifier or turpentine.
Lower Pear	
Undercoat	Above upper pear undercoat shade.
Deepen and shade	Alizaran crimson mixed with burnt sienna (deeper than swatch #25).

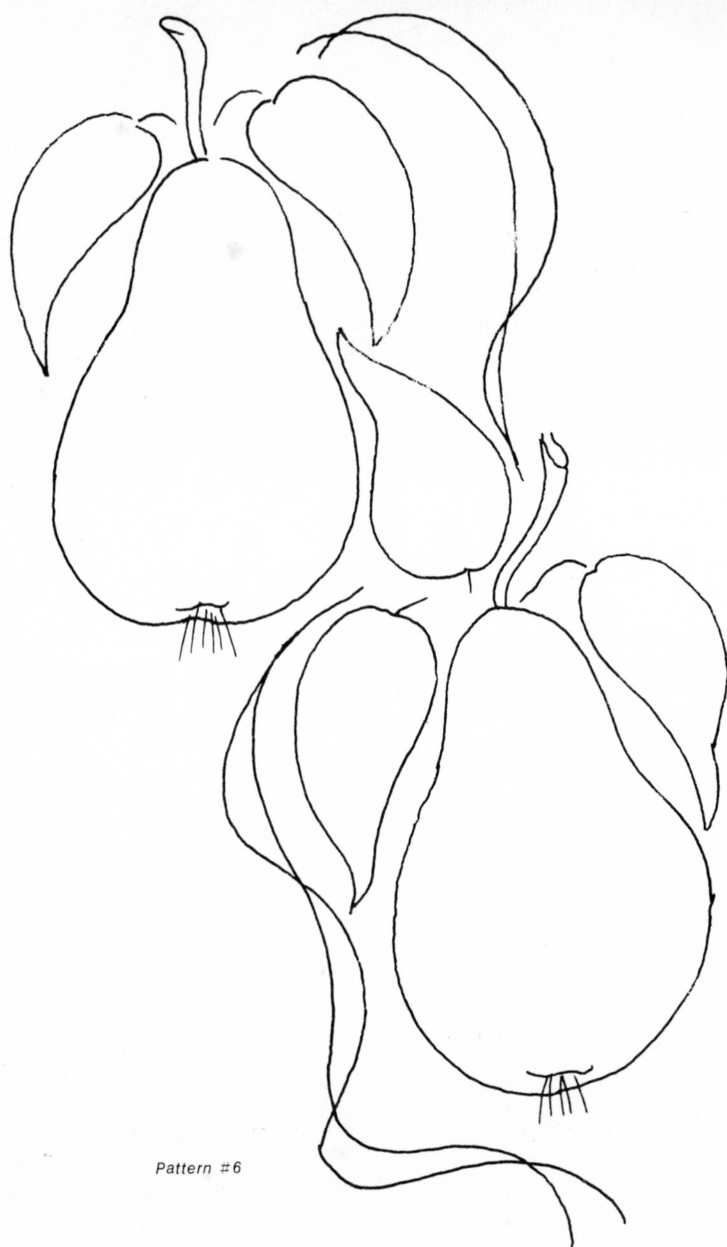
Pattern #6

Lighten and highlight	Titanium white.
Leaves (do not mix until ready to paint)	
Darker shade	Permanent green light mixed with a bit of burnt sienna and titanium white to match swatch #17.
Lighter shade	Titanium white added to some of the above deeper green to match swatch #15.

Lesson Pattern

Pears are the first of many fruits you will begin to paint. After you've learned how to paint several different fruits, you'll be able to put them together to make designs on trays, cannisters, wood and metal boxes, long wooden panels, groupings of miniature panels, cabinets, furniture, and many other objects.

Upper Pear

Begin this lesson by mixing the following colors with the help of the chart.

First, mix the yellow shade used to undercoat both pears. Then add a drop or two (or more, if needed) of modifier or turpentine. Undercoat only the upper pear now and complete the shading before applying the undercoat to the lower pear.

Next, mix the green shade, adding a few drops of copal painting medium. This shade will be used to deepen the left side of the pear. To deepen the right side of the pear, use only a bit of the burnt sienna with a drop of copal.

Now to begin painting: Moisten the large, flat brush in turpentine and squeeze it dry in the lap rag before filling it with the yellow shade. Fill in the entire pear with the yellow shade, painting just inside the fruit outline. Apply the undercoat generously, painting over it a second time if necessary. Whenever you're painting fruit, use a generous amount of paint because dry-brushing, sponging, and blending will remove some of it.

When the undercoating is completed, gently squeeze the brush in the tissue to remove excess paint. Do not clean in turpentine.

Stroke into the edge of the green shade about two or three times, and fill one-fourth of the brush. Begin to paint the green shade at the center top of the pear, keeping this color to the outside and continuing along the left side and halfway across the base. As you apply the green shading, extend the color to the outline of the pear so that the brush will smoothly catch in the undercoat along the outside edges.

Make sure that the shading colors are just moist enough to flow easily with a light brush pressure. Tip the flat brush very slightly to the outside edge as you add the shading color so that the fruit outline is sharp and clear. Wipe the brush frequently to remove any undercoat color that your brush has picked up before again filling with the shading color. The lap rag is very convenient for this quick wiping off of excess paint.

To deepen the right side of the pear, use burnt sienna slightly moistened with copal. Since this is a very strong color, add a small amount to one side of the brush and continue adding this color just as was done for the opposite side of the pear.

When the colors have been added to both sides of the pear, again wipe the brush and get ready to dry-brush and blend the colors together. When using the flat brush for dry-brushing, always use a light touch to whisk the inside edges of the deeper shading colors into the undercoat color. Be sure to wipe the brush frequently to remove the excess paint so that you won't just move it around on the fruit.

Shade from dark to light as you dry-brush, leaving the outside a deeper shade and blending gradually into the lighter center area. Whenever you use the sponge for blending, fold it into a small roll so that you can easily turn to a fresh area frequently. Use the same light whisk for blending with the sponge or cloth.

After the shading is completed, you are ready to add a small highlight in the upper center area or wherever else you may choose. Again, wipe the brush—do not clean it in turpentine.

Thin the titanium white slightly. Using the flat brush, paint a short, slightly curved streak of white to suggest light striking the fruit. It is best to add the highlight when the fruit colors are still moist so that the highlight blends in rather than contrasts.

When the shading is completed, thoroughly clean the brush and sponge in turpentine and squeeze each dry in the lap rag.

As you learn to paint each new fruit, you will find its drying slowly an advantage because this enables you to perfect the shading techniques while the paint remains moist and workable. After you have learned to shade fruits quickly, add drops of dryer or use the spray fixative to hasten the drying time.

Lower Pear

The lower pear is undercoated just as the upper pear, using the same yellow shade. However, it is deepened and shaded with only one shade of darker red.

Apply the red shade as you did for the first pear. One side of the pear should be darker than the other side—this is easily achieved by simply taking an additional stroke or two of the red shade on the darker side of the brush.

When this is completed, use the dry brush or sponge to blend the colors lightly. Leave the center area lighter. Add the white highlight when you have finished shading the pear.

Leaves and Stems

Using your spatula, lift aside the pear colors and mix the two shades of green to be used for the leaves. Always mix white with the leaf colors whether the leaves are to be used with fruit or flowers.

After mixing the two shades of green, set aside a bit of the burnt sienna, which will be used later to deepen the darker green shade and to paint the stems, leaf veins, vine effect, and whiskers at the pear base.

Although pear leaves are longer than those leaves you have previously painted, they will be painted just as the basic leaf was. Keep either the light or darker green to the outside, whichever you prefer or is more attractive for the background color. Add a bit of the burnt sienna to the darker green and thin with drops of turpentine. Using just the tip of the small pointed brush, lightly paint the stems, leaf veins, and winding vine effect.

Paint a thin line of the dark green at the base of the pears. Then add a few light strokes below it to form the whiskers. Use the small pointed brush filled with the two shades of green to paint the stem, painting from the base outward. Take an extra stroke to widen the stem as it ends. Use the dark green to paint an oval line around the stem, placing a spot of white in the center of it to suggest a highlight.

LESSON 4

Daisy-type Flowers

Daisies may be painted in a dozen different shades of blue, pink, off-white, violet, and rust colors. Imagine them in any color you choose and the chances are that Mother Nature has produced them in just that coloring. Although this lesson is painted in the more familiar yellow and orange tones, feel free to substitute other colors for these.

Painting the daisies and leaves of this lesson will give you a chance to use the side and corner of the flat brush. When you have painted a few petals, you will see why it's always necessary to keep your flat brush in good working condition. As you finish using the brush, be sure to clean it thoroughly and reshape it by flattening it between your thumb and index finger. A brush with shaggy, separated ends just won't make a clean, sharp stroke and you'll have two or three stray lines marring your work.

As you have discovered while painting the comma-stroke exercises with the flat brush (see Pattern #2), it is necessary to place the brush at a slight angle to begin the stroke. The beginning angle forces the left (or right) inside corner of the brush to be pressed against the surface, thus allowing the rest of the brush to paint a rounded petal stroke. Pick up the dry, flat brush and collapse the entire brush against the under square corner. From the collapsed position, lean back on the brush until the silver ferrule touches the surface and forces the brush into its widest width. Slowly lift the brush as you paint, tipping it slightly to the right or left until only one square corner remains against the surface to paint a fine line to end the stroke.

Photograph #7

The comma stroke is used for painting daisy petals and some leaves. The stroke can be curved to the right or left, or it can be painted straight down, much like an exclamation point. Since this entire stroke takes only a second to make, practice it in slow motion so that you can watch the brush perform.

The amount of pressure applied to the brush determines the width of each petal. A firm pressure will paint the petals as large as the lesson pattern; a light pressure will paint them much smaller. Experiment, using varying brush pressures for varying sizes.

Look at your pattern a moment, and notice that some of the leaves lie under the daisies. All these underlying leaves will be painted first. The green fill-in flower and the base of the buds are added when the daisies are finished.

Begin this lesson by mixing the colors in the chart. Start by painting the leaves under the daisies. Stroke into the lighter shade of green for half or more of the brush width before adding the deeper shade of green to the opposite side. The open construction of this leaf is shown in Pattern #3.

The short, curved, comma strokes are brushed from the leaf center to the outside. Drop each stroke slightly below the previous stroke and paint each one slightly shorter. Tip the brush to the lower outside corner to point the leaves slightly. These leaves can be as irregular and ragged as you choose. When the leaves are completed, clean the brush in turpentine and use it to paint the daisies next.

Daisy wall plaque. By B. Kay Fraser.

Before painting the daisies, add a few drops of copal painting medium to the yellow and orange shades so that they flow easily. The white can be used with a little thinning (a drop or two).

The painting order you will follow is:

- Paint the yellow daisies; add overtones and shading.
- Paint the orange daisies, add overtones and shading.
- Paint and shade the buds.
- Paint and shade all the daisy centers.
- Paint the fill-in flower.

Brushes

Daisies and leaves	Small flat brush
Stems, veins, and daisy center detail	Small pointed brush

Colors

Daisies	
Yellow	Cadmium yellow medium mixed with a bit of cadmium red light, a bit of viridian green or burnt sienna, and titanium white (similar to swatches #48 and #49).
Orange	Cadmium red light mixed with a bit of burnt sienna and titanium white (similar to swatches #54 and #55).
Daisy centers	
Orange daisies	Yellow.
Yellow daisies	Orange.
Upper highlight	Titanium white.
Lower half	A bit of thinned burnt sienna or cadmium red light, dry-brushed on for added color.
Dark dots below centers	A bit of burnt umber or burnt sienna, thinned with turpentine.
Dark accents in centers	A bit of burnt umber mixed with burnt sienna, or either color used alone, thinned with turpentine.
Light accents in centers	Titanium white.
Buds	Above daisy colors.
Leaves	
Lighter shade	Permanent green light mixed with a bit of burnt sienna and titanium white (similar to swatch #37).
Darker shade	Bit of burnt sienna added to the above green shade (similar to swatch #38). More permanent green light and titanium white added if necessary.

Stems	Burnt umber or burnt sienna added to a little of the above green shade (similar to swatch #18).
Fill-in flower	Green and white or the daisy colors with white.

Lesson Pattern

Daisies

Begin by painting the yellow daisies in the center of Pattern #7. Fill the flat brush with the yellow paint, and stroke each petal from the outside in toward the center. Use the collapsed side of the brush, as described earlier, to begin each petal stroke.

While you paint the daisy, turn the pattern frequently so that you can easily paint a slight curve or droop in some of the petals. About halfway across the daisy, the side petals begin to curve slightly downward while the lower center petals become uncurved and point straight downward. Watch carefully so that your daisy petals won't have a swirled appearance. When petals are completed, wipe the brush in tissue to remove some of the paint.

To add overtones, slide the square edge of the flat brush into the white so that the brush edge is tipped in white. Lightly stroke the white over the damp petal undercoat with the same brush stroke used for the petals. It is not usually necessary to pick up more white for each petal. Let the undercoat help shade as you paint so that all the petals are not exactly alike. Now that the first daisy is painted, go ahead and paint the rest of them—both yellow and orange—in this manner. Remember to complete the shading of each daisy before painting the next one because the undercoat must remain damp in order to help shade the petals.

Pattern #7

Buds

The buds are painted with the narrow side of the flat brush, using the daisy colors and white. Tip one corner of the paint-filled brush into the white and then use the narrow side to make a series of three or four short press-strokes, painting from the outside in.

The green bud bases are painted slightly over the shaded buds, using the same short strokes.

Daisy Centers

Clean the flat brush before painting the daisy centers, using yellow centers in the orange-colored daisies and orange centers in the yellow daisies.

Use a generous amount of paint to fill in the oval centers so that the dry-brushing of white, brown, or red over it will not remove the center color. As the oval centers are painted, the petal ends will be smoothly caught in and connected to the center. When this is completed, lightly wipe the brush in tissue.

To add the white highlight, stroke into the white two or three times, leaving an edge of white on one side of the brush. Keeping the white to the outside, place the brush against the daisy center, painting a long, curved stroke from left to right across the upper half of the center.

Wipe the brush. Add a bit of the thinned cadmium red light to the edge of the brush, and lightly pat and blend it into the lower half of the yellow daisy centers. Use the thinned burnt sienna to pat and blend into the orange-colored daisy centers.

The darker accent around the lower half of the daisies may be dotted in with the corner of the flat brush or the tip of the small pointed brush, using the thinned burnt umber or burnt sienna.

Leaves and Fill-in Flower

The shaded-leaf effect below the large center daisy and beside the buds is painted with the narrow side of the brush as was done in the open construction of the basic leaves (Pattern #3). Paint the longest stroke from the outside in to the stem, followed by gradually shorter strokes.

The fill-in flower is added last, using either a shade of green and white or the daisy shades and white.

Optional Method

An alternate method of painting daisies, which you might like to try next, is the one-stroke shaded petal. Fill half, or a little more, of the brush with the daisy color and the remainder with white. As you paint, keep the white side of the brush to the outside of the petal curve, adding more color and white after two or three strokes. If you want to experiment with painting a ragged-type daisy, try stroking from the center of the flower to the outside of the petal.

LESSON 5

Apples

The red apple you paint in this lesson is the first of several different red shadings you will be learning to mix and combine for other red fruit. In mixing the shades, add drops of both the super dryer and the copal painting medium if necessary. Add the dryer first. You will need to experiment to find the number of drops needed. If it needs further thinning, add copal painting medium. Count the number of drops of each that you add to each color. This will help you learn just how little you can use to adjust for your altitude and climate. High altitudes require more dryer.

Brushes

Apples and leaves	Large flat brush
Stems and all fine detail	Small pointed brush

Colors

Upper apple	
Undercoat	Grumbacher red.
Deepen and shade	Grumbacher red mixed with burnt umber for a deep oxblood color. deep oxblood color.
Lighten	Titanium white mixed with cadmium yellow medium to match swatch #21.
Highlight	A bit of titanium white on the tip of the spatula.
Lower Apple	
Undercoat	Titanium white mixed with cadmium yellow medium to match swatch #20.
Deepen and shade	Permanent green light mixed with burnt umber and titanium white, added bit by bit, to match swatch #17.
Lighten and highlight	Titanium white.
Leaves (do not mix until ready to paint)	
Darker shade	Permanent green light mixed with burnt umber and titanium white to match swatch #18.
Lighter shade	A little cadmium yellow medium, more permanent green light, burnt umber, and titanium white added to the above shade to match swatch #17.
Stems, veins, and other fine details	Deeper shade of green mixed with a bit more burnt umber if necessary.

Photograph #8

Lesson Pattern

Upper Apple

Begin by mixing the colors for the upper apple. Always moisten the brush in turpentine and squeeze it dry before filling with the paint. Then, fill the large flat brush with the Grumbacher red, which has been thinned slightly.

Paint just inside the outline of the apple with red paint and then fill in the entire apple. Paint over the apple a second time, if necessary, to cover thoroughly the background color you will be decorating upon later. When this is completed, wipe your brush in the tissue and fill one-third (or up to one-half) of the flat brush with the oxblood shade. The amount of this deeper shading oxblood color added will determine how bright or how dark the finished apple will appear.

Use a very light brush pressure to add the shading color. Begin at the center top and extend the deeper color to the outline. This will not only accent the outer edges but smoothly catch in the sides of the fruit for a smoothly blended effect. As you continue around the apple, you will need to wipe the brush frequently to remove the red paint before adding more of the deeper red. As you accent the tips of the apples, you may find it easier to turn the clipboard upside down, brushing the deeper color slightly up into the apple. To paint one side of the apple deeper than the opposite side, just take one or two extra, slightly curved strokes along that particular side.

When you have finished adding the deeper shading color, thoroughly wipe the brush in the tissue and lap rag before you begin dry-brushing.

Use very light pressure on the brush as you blend and dry-brush the colors together, following the contour of the fruit. Whenever you are dry-brushing, be sure to wipe the brush frequently with the lap rag.

To lighten the apple, use the very pale yellow shade #21, adding only a drop or two of turpentine or copal painting medium to thin it. Squeeze the brush thoroughly before picking up the pale yellow shade. Pat a generous amount of this shade over the lighter center area. Again, wipe the brush in the tissue or lap rag and gently dry-brush the pale yellow into the red undercoat. Add more pale yellow if you need more light contrast.

Now you are ready to add a highlight, but do not clean your brush yet. Just squeeze it in the tissue before picking up a little of the slightly thinned titanium white. One light, short, and slightly curved brush stroke is usually enough to form a highlight. Clean the brush in turpentine and put it aside.

The wide-spread U at the base of the stem should be painted next. (The stem will be added when you paint the leaves.) Using only the tip of the small pointed brush, paint the U, letting each end fade into the deeper red of the apple. Use the deep oxblood red, adding more brown if necessary for added contrast and a little turpentine to thin it. Gently wipe the brush and pick up a little of the pale yellow shade. Pat and blend this shade into the lower center area behind the U. This will contrast the light against the dark well and will also pave the way for adding the stem later.

Lower Apple

The green apple is painted in the same manner as the red apple but with different colors. Use the spatula to lift aside any of the remaining red shades, mix the suggested shades of yellow and green for the second apple, and paint the green apple just as you did the red.

When you have finished painting, wrap any remaining oil colors in an airtight square of waxed paper and use later. If you are using a glass palette, place waxed paper directly over the oil colors and remove it when you are ready to paint again.

Leaves and Stems

The leaves are painted with the large flat brush, using the two suggested shades of green. Paint these just as you have painted the basic leaves. The leaf stems and veins are painted with a deeper shade of green and thinned with drops of turpentine. Using just the tip of the small pointed brush, lightly paint in these details.

The stems for both apples also are painted with the small pointed brush and thinned paint. To paint the stems, use two shades—either dark and light green or dark green and light brown—for a blended stroke. Paint a small oval of brown or green at the stem ending and place a spot of white in the center of it. You may also want to add some white to highlight the center of the stem. Dry-brush lightly.

Pattern #8

Photograph #9

LESSON 6

Hummingbird

You will be painting this hummingbird considerably larger than life size in order to learn to make shaded strokes using the smaller—and easier—brush. As you progress, you will be able to paint these dainty birds nearer to their natural size with very small flat brushes. Whether you are a bird watcher or not, you will have fun watching this fellow come to life under your brush!

Brushes

Bird body and wings, blossoms and leaves	Small flat brush
Bird beak, stems, and blossom centers	Small pointed brush

Colors

Wings	
Darker shade	Ivory black mixed with titanium white for a deep charcoal shade.
Lighter shade	Titanium white added to some of the above charcoal shade for a light gray shade.
Head, back, and center tail feathers	Permanent green light mixed with cadmium yellow medium, raw umber, a bit of ivory black, and titanium white (similar to swatch #39).
Chest undercoat	Titanium white, dry-brushed with gray.
Throat	
Lighter shade	Cadmium red light mixed with a bit of burnt sienna and titanium white (similar to swatch #54).

Darker shade	Burnt sienna added to some of the above shade for a slightly deeper shade.
Beak	Ivory black, thinned with turpentine or copal painting medium.
Mask	Deep charcoal shade used for the wings.
Eye	Titanium white.
Blossoms	Above red shade #54 mixed with titanium white and a bit of ivory black for a pale pink shade.
Leaves	
Lighter shade	Above green shade #39.
Darker shade	Burnt umber added to some of the above shade.
Twigs	Above shade edged in white.

Lesson Pattern

Wings

When you have mixed the contrasting shades of gray and dark charcoal, begin to paint the wings. Use the small flat brush to stroke first into the lighter gray, filling half (or a little more) of the brush. Turn the unfilled portion of the brush into the edge of the deeper charcoal shade, taking fewer strokes of this shade to fill the brush.

Pattern #9

Paint the wings with the light gray shade to the outside and the darker charcoal to the inside. Begin the strokes from the outside tip of the wings to the inside, painting the longer feathers first and continuing in toward the body. Using the same colors, stroke in the shorter feathers on top of the wings and the left and right tail feathers. Clean the brush whenever necessary to prevent the two colors from merging into one shade.

Head, Back, and Center Tail Feathers

Mix the green shade #39 to paint the head and back. As you paint the center tail feathers, add a little charcoal beside the green and paint from the outside in toward the body.

With a little green in the brush, tip one corner of the flat brush into the charcoal shade. Lightly pivot the charcoal-filled tip of the brush here and there to suggest feathers over the back.

Chest

Clean the brush and fill with white to undercoat the chest. Wipe the brush before picking up a little of the gray shade, and lightly dry-brush the gray over the damp undercoat. Accent the lower, outside area with a little of the charcoal shade and lightly dry-brush into the gray.

Throat

Clean the brush, fill with the lighter red shade, and paint the throat. When this is finished, pick up a little of the deeper red on one corner of the brush and blend into the outside edge of the throat.

Beak, Mask, and Eye

Thin the black with drops of turpentine or copal painting medium, and use the small pointed brush to paint the beak, stroking from the outside in toward the head. Then clean the brush and use it to paint the mask in the deep charcoal shade. Adding a bit of white to the brush, work a small oval of gray into the charcoal shade. Add a small dot of pure white to the center of the eye. Clean the brush and put it aside.

Blossoms and Leaves

Paint the blossoms with the small flat brush, using the remaining red shade mixed with white for a pleasing light pink shade. Fill the brush with the pink shade and edge each side in white. Paint the petals with the press-stroke.

Add a little yellow to the centers of each blossom and accent the edge with charcoal or green. Paint the leaves with the small flat brush, using the two suggested shades of green, and paint the twigs with the small pointed brush, using the deeper shade of green with white for a shaded effect. Use the deeper green shade to add the stems.

Hummingbird lesson pattern on a decorative watering can. By Yee Chea Lin.

Photograph #10

LESSON 7

Peaches

The pear- and apple-painting lessons were concerned mainly with learning the steps necessary to paint fruit and the shading effects obtained by applying various colors over wet undercoat shades. This lesson will concentrate on the shading necessary to separate and distinguish one fruit from another when they are in groups and clusters. Unless they are shaded and separated, they'll merely seem like blobs of color. To paint good-looking fruit arrangements, the fruits must always overlap.

Before you mix your paint, look closely at both your pattern and the color photograph. You will notice that the lower peach is partially hidden by the upper peach. This is the beginning point—the peach that is underneath. Whenever overlapped fruit, flowers, or leaves are to be painted, always complete the one underneath first.

One thing more. Have your sponge handy because you will use it frequently in this lesson. If you haven't already cut your sponge into small pieces—about 1 inch square—do so now. If the sponge is too large, it will extend beyond the fruit as you shade it, causing a smeared edge. Squeeze it together between your fingers, turning it frequently to the unused portions, as you blend. After the sponge has picked up paint, squeeze it in turpentine before the paint dries, and again squeeze it firmly in your lap rag to remove excess turpentine. Should you forget to clean the sponge when you are finished and find that the paint has hardened in it, snip off the hard spots with scissors.

Brushes

Undercoat and leaves	Large flat brush
Stems	Large pointed brush
Leaf veins	Small pointed brush

Colors

Peaches

Undercoat	Cadmium yellow medium mixed with titanium white to match swatch #19, thinned with turpentine. (Later

Pattern #10

	you may like to experiment with the yellow just as it is—adding no white.)
Deepen and shade	A bit of cadmium red light mixed with a bit of alizaran crimson and a bit of burnt sienna (deeper than swatch #1), thinned with turpentine. (For this particular shading we find that burnt sienna works more effectively when it is used almost full strength.)
Lighten and highlight	Titanium white.
Leaves	Permanent green light.

Lesson Pattern

Peaches

As for all fruit, the first step is to undercoat. Using the large flat brush, undercoat the underneath peach first, painting just a fraction inside the outline. This is done partially because the fruit will "grow" a little as you add the darker and lighter colors and partially because the darker shade will be more distinct if there is no undercoat beneath it.

Go ahead and undercoat the top peach now if you like, but don't shade it until the underneath peach is shaded and completely finished. The third small peach should be painted after you have finished the upper two. You don't have to worry about your hand brushing into the wet undercoat if it is painted last. As you become a more experienced decorator, dodging fresh paint will become quite easy. All leaves and stems will be painted after the peaches have been completed.

In the future, when you are painting fruit, undercoat all the fruit you expect to shade and finish at one time. Should you be interrupted long enough for the undercoat to dry out, just apply a fresh undercoat over the top and continue with the shading steps.

Now mix the paints for step two—the deepen-and-shade step. Your brush will be full of yellow paint, but don't clean it in turpentine. Simply gently wipe the excess paint in the tissue or lap rag, as you want a little of the yellow paint to remain in the brush.

Take another look at the colored photograph, and notice that the reason these two peaches look separated is the contrast of dark against light. Whenever one fruit overlaps another, you must plan to paint the darker area of one fruit against the lighter area of the other. In this lesson keep the darker shades to the right, gradually lightening the peach on the left side.

Stroke into the edge of the red mixture once or twice, using about one-third of the brush width. Tip the same corner of the brush into the burnt sienna and press lightly as you add it beside the red mixture. Turn the brown to the outside of your brush, red inside, and beginning at the upper right, lightly outline the underneath peach. Continue this shading halfway around, or a little more if you choose. By this time, most of the red and brown will have been deposited on the peach, but enough usually remains to color the left side slightly. Just turn over the brush and continue to outline the left side. If there isn't enough color there to please you, pick up a bit of the red mixture (no brown), and blend it into the left side. You may want to deepen further the right side by dry-brushing a bit more of the brown or of the red and brown together over your first shading.

Now blend these shades together by dry-brushing lightly or by sponging. You will do both in this lesson. Squeeze the paint from your brush and lightly blend the shading colors into the yellow undercoat, following the rounded edges of the peach. Leave the center area of the peach yellow for now. Again, squeeze the paint from your brush, and lay it aside for a few moments.

Using the sponge, gently pat and blend again. If you get into the yellow center a bit, it won't matter at all. It should begin to look like a fuzzy peach now. You will add more fuzz a little later.

Now that you have sponged and blended the shading colors so that they lighten as they approach the center of the peach, you're ready to use the brush again to paint in a division, or bulge, line. You may not want all your fruit to have a bulge, but you will learn how to paint them in this lesson so that you can decide. Before painting, be sure that some of the yellow undercoat is showing. This bit of yellow will give depth, as the deeper shade is painted just inside it.

Using one corner of the brush, pick up a tip of the red mixture first and then a tip of the brown on the same corner. Follow Pattern #10 for these first bulges; later, you will be able to paint them without the guide lines. Place the paint-filled corner of the brush near the stem, and stroke, lightly curving it so that it blends into the lower area of the fruit. Now sponge again for a gentle blending, lightly patting the bulge if it should seem too harsh or pronounced.

The last step is to lighten and highlight. In this case, this step will give the peach the final textured, fuzzy appearance. Clean your brush in turpentine and squeeze it dry. Add a drop or two of clean turpentine to titanium white and mix it with your spatula. With your brush, generously pat on the white in the center area of the peach. Use the sponge, as directed before, in a series of gentle pats. Be sure that your final pats are a bit rounded and that all shades blend, leaving no distinct bands of color. Sponging does an ideal job of blending, sometimes better than a brush. If you want to highlight the peach a little more, use the flat side of the brush to pat on a spot or two of white.

The top or overlapping peach is now ready to be shaded just as the underneath peach was painted. The darker shading colors will begin at the upper right and will be dark enough to contrast with the lighter center of the underneath peach. Just remember "dark against light" whenever you paint groups of fruit, and they will always come out looking beautiful.

Leaves and Stems

There are no set colors that leaves must be painted, so feel free to paint them in your own choice of shades. Use two or three shades on the brush with light and dark contrasts. To soften a leaf color, add a bit of the red shade used in this lesson. This warms the leaf color and ties the fruit and leaves together.

The peach leaf is constructed just as the first basic leaf was and is painted as the leaf in the pear lesson was, using a long, flowing stroke. By now you have had lots of practice painting this type of leaf so that you should find it quite easy to do. Either the flat or pointed brush can be used, whichever is the easiest.

The stems and leaf veins are painted with the small pointed brush or just the tip of the large pointed brush. A bit of burnt umber or burnt sienna may be added to the dark green shade for the stems, twigs, and leaf veins. The stem can be painted as it was in the apple lesson.

LESSON 8

Lilacs

You will notice that this lesson's color photograph introduces two quite different shadings. If you want to change the color scheme of this lesson to please your individual tastes or room decor, all you need do is vary the undercoat color. By adding white to dilute the undercoat shade or raw umber to deepen it, you will have several different shades, all of which will be pretty. After this lesson, try an entirely different undercoat shade—such as a shade similar to swatch #10 or #11. Remember to use two shades of undercoat, a dark shade and a lighter shade.

Brushes

Lilac undercoat and large leaves	Large flat brush
Blossom petals and small leaves	Small flat brush
Flower centers and fine detail	Small pointed brush

Colors

Upper lilac	Cobalt violet mixed with alizaran crimson and enough titanium white to match swatch #4; more titanium white added to some of above shade to match swatch #6.

Lower lilac (do not mix until ready to paint)	Cobalt violet mixed with titanium white to match swatch #31; Prussian blue mixed with titanium white to match swatch #8.
Blossoms	Titanium white mixed with cadmium yellow medium to match swatch #20; ivory black.
Leaves and stems	Permanent green light mixed with titanium white to match swatch #39; burnt umber mixed with raw umber and titanium white to match swatch #52.

Photograph #11

Lesson Pattern
Lilac Undercoat

Now you will apply the undercoat using a different method—dabbling. Just fill the large flat brush with paint matching swatch #4, and dabble the color generously down the middle of the lilac outline (Pattern #11). Round it out more at the top and sides, and narrow it at the end in a ragged oval shape. You need a heavy undercoat here, so don't be stingy. The oval of color should be about 1/4 inch inside the outline.

Clean the brush and fill it with swatch #6 for more dabbling. The next step is to surround the oval with the lighter shade. Dabble this color beyond the lilac outline about 1/8 inch (or more if you want a larger lilac). Try to be careless as you dabble. The flower will be far prettier if you have an irregular undercoat edge instead of a precise cone shape. As you dabble the outside undercoat color, turn the brush in little swoops to produce a ragged-edge effect.

Just one more step and the undercoat will be finished. With the lighter shade in your brush, lightly dabble the edge where the two undercoat shades meet, so that there is a slight blending of colors. You can eliminate this step on your next lilac: As you circle the

Pattern #11

cone of color with the contrasting shade, just slightly overlap the cone here and there as you dabble the brush. Remember that you don't want two perfect ovals of color, neatly and precisely painted, so feel free to be a little messy.

Clean your brush, mix new paints, and follow the same instructions for the lower lilac. When you finish, clean your brush and replace it in your brush container.

Blossoms

Paint the blossoms with the small flat brush, using only white to form the petals over the wet undercoat. Stroke into the edge of the white just once or twice, and paint the petals in groups of four over the entire cone of darker color. As you did in Lesson 2, form this small blossom by lightly pressing down the square end of the flat brush and then lifting up. This particular flower doesn't require a stroke. The brush shape and the wet undercoat work for you, shaping and blending each petal automatically. You'll probably find that after two petals have been formed, you'll need to pick up more white to complete the group. Don't clean your brush; just wipe it over the tissue to remove any accumulation of dark undercoat. There's no need to be particular that every petal is very white; the undercoat will do the shading for you. Each petal should show a slightly heavier deposit of white to the outside, shading lighter to the inside. Sometimes you may want to overlap a few blossoms—then you'll need a grouping of only three petals.

Clean the brush in turpentine and go on to paint the petals over the outside, lighter shade of the cone. Begin this layer of petals at the joining of the two undercoat shades. As you paint, you will notice that some of the lighter shade will blend with the darker shade, so that the dark center gradually blends into the lighter sides and there is a very light shade to the outer sides.

To finish the lilac and give it a fluffy, delicate appearance, add a few petals—a little smaller and in groups of two or three—beyond the outline at the trailing ends of the lilac. To connect and finish the top and side sprigs, pick up both light and dark shades plus white and add the final petals. You will need only a bit of yellow and a bit of black, softened in a drop or two of turpentine, to dot the blossom centers. Using the small pointed brush, first dot in the yellow and then add a smaller dot of black beside each yellow dot.

Leaves and Stems

In this pattern the leaves can be painted either before or after the lilac is completed. If you paint them last, you may want to add a few more blossoms right over the leaves, snuggled down in the stem area. Swatch shades #39 and #52 were used for the leaf shades in the photograph. Combining green with shades of warm brown, as we did for these shades, gives a very soft and effective shading. You may add more white to these shades for an even more delicate coloring, or you may prefer to use one of the brighter green shades shown in the swatch chart. Use the small pointed brush and either the green or brown shade for the stem and twig effect. Keep the paint very thin for these fine lines.

The larger leaves are painted with the large flat brush, following the directions for the basic leaf. Fill about three-fourths of the brush with the green shade and the remaining edge with brown. Then stroke the brush once or twice on the palette so that the colors blend slightly. The green is kept to the inside of the leaf and the brown to the outside, but this may be varied as desired for certain background colors. You might also like to add some white to the green and brown already on your brush for a triple-toned leaf. Just slide the brush into the edge of the white, stroking through only once or twice, and paint your leaf in the three shades.

Each of the small leaves on this pattern is painted using only one stroke and the same leaf color. These small leaves can be painted almost like a blossom petal except that they are painted from the stem out, ending in a point. Press the brush down to form the point of the leaf. (The brush will be moved only very slightly to paint these and not at all if you paint very tiny leaves.) The small leaves can be made to curve in either direction. This leaf is called the mustache leaf because its shape resembles just that—a mustache, which is larger at the inside and twirls to outside points. One word of caution, though—don't try to capture the perfect balance of a mustache. Drop one leaf below the other for a graceful effect.

The one-stroke leaf is used frequently in decorative painting. You'll be painting these small leaves again, next time with rosebuds, so practice them. Practice the triple-toned leaf too, using the large flat brush. Perfecting it will save you lots of time and give a very pretty effect. In fact, many of the commercial hand-decorated objects use this leaf motif, with flowers, almost entirely.

Photograph #12

LESSON 9

Strawberries

In past fruit-painting lessons, you painted large fruits like pears, apples, and peaches. Now you're ready to start on smaller fruit, having learned to be dexterous with the flat brush. Strawberries are fun to paint, and you'll enjoy painting them in not just one color but in *many* colors.

Brushes

Strawberry undercoat, strawberries, and large leaves	Large flat brush
Stems, curliques, and seeds	Small pointed brush

Colors

Red strawberries	
Undercoat	Cadmium red light, softened in turpentine.
Deepen and shade	Alizaran crimson mixed with burnt umber for a deep oxblood shade.
Lighten and highlight	Cadmium yellow medium mixed with titanium white to match swatch #21.
Seeds	Ivory black, softened in turpentine; cadmium yellow medium, softened in turpentine.
Green strawberry	
Undercoat	Light leaf-green shade following.
Deepen and shade	Red strawberry shade above.
Leaves (do not mix until ready to paint)	
Dark leaf	Permanent green light mixed with titanium white and a

	bit of the above oxblood shade (similar to swatch #38).
Light leaf	Titanium white mixed with some of the above shade (similar to swatch #37).
Stems and curliques	A bit more burnt umber added to the darker green shade for a slightly deeper shade.

Lesson Pattern

Red Strawberries

Undercoat the strawberries with the red, which has been softened in turpentine. As you did in the previous fruit-painting lessons, completely outline and fill in the berry. When this is finished, wipe the brush lightly in tissue. Add a few drops of turpentine to the oxblood shade so that it will flow easily. With the large flat brush, stroke into this shade once or twice, allowing no more than one-fourth of the brush to pick up the deeper shade. At the upper left of the strawberry, begin to add the deeper shade along the side and around the bottom. By now your brush will probably have gotten dry. If you lightly wipe it on the tissue and turn it over, there will be enough color in the brush to continue around the strawberry with a slightly lighter shade of the oxblood.

Now you're ready to dry-brush and blend the deeper shades into the strawberry. Squeeze the brush in the tissue or wipe dry and then use to lightly blend the brown into the red. You will notice that there is a slight "bulge" in the strawberry, which adds dimension.

Pattern #12

In order to bring out this bulge, brush out a little more of the brown so that a little of the red undercoat shows through. Again, pick up the oxblood shade on one corner of the brush and lightly paint a slight curve in this area. Wipe the brush in the tissue or lap rag, and blend the curved stroke into the strawberry so that the center area remains lighter. Clean the brush in turpentine and squeeze dry.

To lighten, fill the brush with the pale yellow mixture and pat it on the strawberry in the center area. This can be applied by dry-brushing or by lightly sponging. As you have just seen, the amount of deeper shading picked up on the brush corner determines the final strawberry coloring. Using a small amount of the darker color on just a few hairs of the brush will produce a brighter berry. A darker strawberry will result if more of the brush is filled with the deeper shade. The very pale yellow added to lighten this strawberry is the final touch needed to give it a special glow.

Paint the other strawberries in exactly the same manner except for the little green strawberry at the bottom of the pattern. You will notice that all the strawberries are darker on the left, lighter on the right, and highlighted in the center area. Feel free to reverse this shading if you choose. You may even wish to paint several shades of strawberries in one arrangement. And remember—when you want to give dimension to a strawberry or any other fruit, you must leave a small amount of the undercoat shade showing just before the darker curved bulge is painted in.

After these are completed, clean your brush thoroughly and put it aside.

Leaves and Stems

The leaves, which are similar to those in the daisy lesson, are painted with the same large flat brush you used for the strawberries. First, fill the brush about half full with the lighter shade. Then stroke through the deeper shade to completely fill the brush. Begin at the center of the leaf, stroking to the outside and ending with a slightly jagged stroke. Continue the second stroke under the first in the same manner until you have completed one side of the leaf. Keeping the dark to the outside, reverse your brush, again stroking from the inside out, slightly dropping each petal a little lower until you have finished four strokes on the leaf. (It isn't necessary that you always paint four strokes—if you use three strokes instead, the effect will be just as pretty. You may also prefer to use the pointed brush—either one will work very well for this lesson.)

After you have completed all the leaves, you're ready to add the strawberry bracts. Since these are most easily painted with the tip of the pointed brush, clean the flat brush and lay it aside. Get out the larger pointed brush and fill it with the darker and the lighter shades of green. Beginning at the center stem line, bring the stroke right over the strawberry to form a little leaf beginning at the top and diminishing to a point in another comma stroke. You will notice that your brush has picked up red from the still-wet strawberry. Wipe it frequently in the tissue to remove the red as you complete the next bract on the strawberry and one or two above it.

The stem will be added next. Now is a time to use a spray to dry the strawberry before the green is applied. Commercially, spraying is done to hasten drying and also to get a finished seal on the object. All your painting should be sealed with either a brush-on varnish or a spray-on fixative. You may prefer the fixative since it acts much more quickly and is just as permanent. It is particularly advantageous in a lesson such as this where the fruit color has been painted in straight oil color and will be slow to dry.

Standing about a foot away, give a very light spray of fixative to the fruit. Wait a few minutes and reapply. In about five or ten minutes, the strawberry will be dry enough for you to add the strawberry bracts without danger of picking up the red. If you don't use the fixative, be sure to wipe your brush after each stroke to remove the red that has accumulated.

Green Strawberry

Now that the red strawberries and the green leaves are completed, drop down to the little green strawberry at the bottom of the pattern. Use the lighter shade of green to undercoat this strawberry. Wipe the brush in tissue, pick up the deeper oxblood shade on one corner of the brush, and lightly dry-brush on a few accents of red. Streak this lightly to give the effect of a green strawberry turning slightly red. Again use the pointed brush to add the strawberry bracts. When this is finished, clean your brush thoroughly and put it aside.

Curliques, Stems, and Seeds

Use the small pointed brush for the curliques, the vine effect, the stem, the veins in the leaves, and the seeds. To add the seeds to the strawberries, soften the black with a few drops of turpentine (or add a little of your red-and-brown mixture to the black). This paint should be very thin and applied with only the tip of the brush. Be a little cautious when adding the strawberry seeds—they are easy to overdo, and not too many are needed to give a seed effect. With black, paint tiny long dots here and there over the berry. To make the seeds seem lighter on the center area, paint a small long dot of yellow right beside the black one. Generally, the strawberry seeds are dark on the dark side and light on the light side. When this is finished, clean the small brush before using it for the next color.

For the curliques and stems, add a little burnt umber to the darker shade of green and thin it with turpentine. You will need this mixture quite thin for easy handling. Using only the tip of the small brush, lightly paint in the stems and leaf veins. Paint the stem from inside the strawberry to the outside, accenting the end with a little darker shade. When this is finished, moisten the tip of the small pointed brush and apply the curliques freehand. Don't attempt to follow the pattern exactly. It will be softer and more graceful if you paint this on your own. Keep your paint quite thin, wrist and arm flexible. Relax—and they will be easy to paint.

Decorative oilcan with strawberries and apple. By Yee Chea Lin.

Photograph #13

LESSON 10

Zinnias

Look at Pattern #13 for a moment. Notice that the leaves are snuggled in quite close to the zinnia. Whenever leaves are very near to the flower, the leaves are usually painted first and the flower extended over them a bit. While you mix the flower colors, the leaves will have time to almost dry. If not, you can spray them dry with a fixative.

In this particular lesson, first paint the zinnias, then the leaves, and the fill-in flower last. Try placing your brush as near the zinnia as possible when you paint the leaves. Since you'll use the large pointed brush for the leaves, you'll be able to use the point to good advantage as you start the leaf stroke.

To refresh your memory on the exercises you will be using to make this zinnia, refer to Patterns #1 and #2, lines c, f, and i. These lines all demonstrate the pivot stroke. Especially good to refresh your memory is line f because it shows the continuous flow of the shaded stroke, which you will be using in the zinnia.

Brushes

Zinnias and fill-in flower	Large flat brush
Leaves and buds	Large pointed brush
Twigs and veins	Small pointed brush

Colors

Zinnias

Deep pink	Alizaran crimson mixed with burnt sienna and titanium white (similar to swatch #28).
Lighter pink	Titanium white added to a bit of the above shade (similar to swatch #28).
Violet	Cobalt violet mixed with a bit of alizaran crimson and titanium white to match swatch #4.
Lighter violet	Titanium white added to some of the above color to match swatch #6.

Zinnia buds	Cobalt violet shaded with titanium white.
Zinnia centers	Cadmium yellow medium; titanium white; viridian green.
Fill-in flowers	Zinnia shades and titanium white.
Leaves	
Lighter shade	Permanent green light mixed with burnt sienna and titanium white to match swatch #17.
Darker shade	Permanent green light mixed with burnt sienna and titanium white to match swatch #19.
Stems and veins	Viridian green.

Lesson Pattern

Pink Zinnias

First, fill your flat brush with the deep pink. Stroke two or three times through the edge of some white until you see a slight shading on your palette. Begin the stroke at the outside of the zinnia at any point you wish. Without lifting your brush from the pattern, continue this stroke in a curve, up and down, and continue into a second or a third curve, or pivot. By this time, you will need to replenish your paint color, so pick up the deeper shade of pink, stroke into the white, and resume painting around the zinnia until you have completed the outer edge.

Wipe the brush in tissue and pick up the lighter shade of pink, again stroking into the white two or three times, leaving a small edge of white on the brush. Place the second row of petals in the zinnia, wherever possible, between the first layer that you have just

Pattern #13

painted. Your zinnia won't be quite so stilted and stiff if you stagger some of the rows of petals. Paint this just as you did the outer row.

After about two or three strokes, again pick up the lighter shade of pink, stroking into the white, and continue with the pivot until the second row is completed. Pick up the lighter shade of pink yet again, stroking into the white a little more so that a slightly lighter shade will be used for the third row of petals, still leaving a small white edge to separate it from the previous row of petals. This final row of petals in the center should be a little bit lighter; this is done by stroking into the white a little more and by leaving a small edge of white showing that will separate the rows of petals.

Continue with the second zinnia in the same shades and in the same manner. When finished, clean the brush thoroughly and fill it with the deeper shade of violet, stroking into the white two or three times for a slight shading and a small white edge.

Violet Zinnias

Begin painting at the outer edge of the flower, encircling the zinnia completely with the deeper shade. Wipe or clean the brush and pick up the lighter shade of violet. Stroke through the white two or three times for a light shading and a small white edge. Again, place a second row of petals at a point that is not exactly in line with the first row of petals so that it has a softer look. Continue around the zinnia with this shade. The third row will be slightly lighter. Simply stroke into the white two or three times until a lighter shade emerges, with a slight edge of white remaining on the brush to separate the third from the second row of petals. Continue in the pivot motion until the third row is complete. Stroke into the white again, picking up a small white edge, and finish the fourth (and center) row of the zinnia. You can add more rows just so long as you keep them separated with a little white.

Leaves

Use the large pointed brush for the leaves. Since you have not used this brush recently, refresh your memory on how to fill it: Stroke into the deeper shade of green with a very firm pressure, forcing it to splay out and drink up the paint. To half fill the brush, you will need to stroke into the darker paint eight or ten times. Do the same with the lighter shade of green, stroking through eight or ten times to completely fill it.

Now you will try something a little different in leaf shading. Fill the brush with the dark and lighter green as usual, and paint half of the leaf. With the two shades of green still in the brush, stroke the lighter side of the brush into the edge of the white several times. With the lighter shade to the outside of the brush, complete the other half of the leaf. This will produce a very pretty leaf, shaded from dark to light to very light. You won't need to clean your brush after each leaf is finished if you squeeze out excess paint in the tissue. You will be able to paint two or three leaves in this manner before it is necessary to clean your brush and start again. This is a good way to add variety to your shades, and it's prettier to soften the greens somewhat by adding white to them for the lighter side.

Buds

When you have completed all the large green leaves, paint the petals on the buds. Using only the tip of your pointed brush, make small basic-stroke commas. Paint the two outside ones from the center top to the outside. The center small one is painted from the stem line slightly down over the bud. There will be three shaded strokes on each bud (or two, if you prefer). When you have finished with the large pointed brush, clean it thoroughly and put it aside.

Flower Centers and Twigs

Use the small pointed brush to paint in the twig effect around the fill-in flower and the centers of the zinnias. The zinnia centers are painted with a very pale yellow and plotted in lightly with the point of the small brush, accenting the outside area with a bit of the green shade and a few dots of white.

Thin the darker green paint, to which you may add a little burnt sienna for a slightly deeper green. This should be quite thin, almost like water. Using only the tip of the small pointed brush, lightly paint the twig effect. Don't bear down with a hard, full line. These should be very wispy and delicate—just a suggestion of a twig effect around the fill-in flower trailing off to almost nothing at each side. When this is completed, clean the brush, put it aside, and pick up the large flat brush again.

Fill-in Flower

Fill *only* one corner of the flat brush, using first the pink and then the white (right on top of the pink). Lightly dot in the fill-in flower, adding white as necessary, to delicately trail off to almost nothing at the ends, just as you did in Lesson 2. Use a pink shade in combination with white at the top of this pattern and the two shades of violet at each side.

LESSON 11

Ribbons and Bows

Ribbons and bows are appealing to most of us, and their use in decorative painting is almost endless. A gay bow or ribbon suggests happiness or a special occasion, which is the reason ribbons and bows often adorn invitations and announcements and are used as party decorations. They are especially right when painted in combination with floral, fruit, or vegetable arrangements, and on anything ranging from small pin and pill boxes to large storage chests, furniture, and walls. There are many uses for painted ribbons and bows—both fluffy and tailored—on objects that you will be decorating in the future.

You will paint two types of ribbons and bows in this lesson, using both the large pointed and the large or small flat brushes. The first bow is a real quickie to paint—just two shaded strokes form each side of the bow and a touch of the brush forms the knot (see diagram). This bow is often used when just the suggestion of a bow is desired.

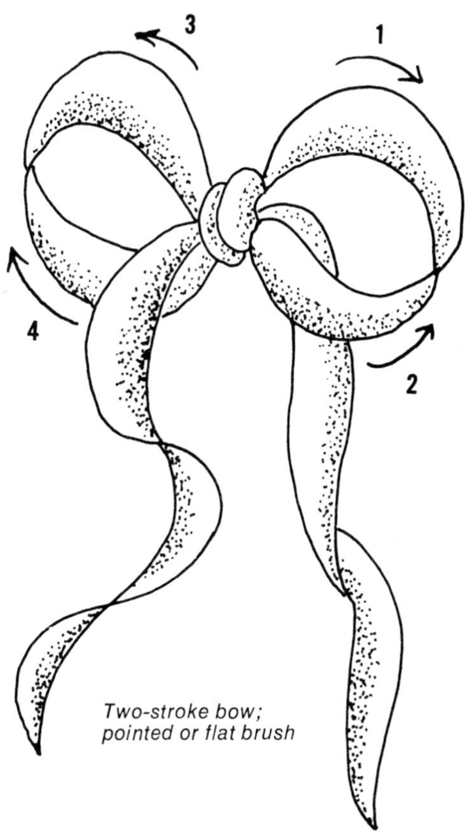

Two-stroke bow; pointed or flat brush

The second type of bow is painted with *three* shaded strokes forming each side, giving the effect of a curved or turned bow (see diagram).

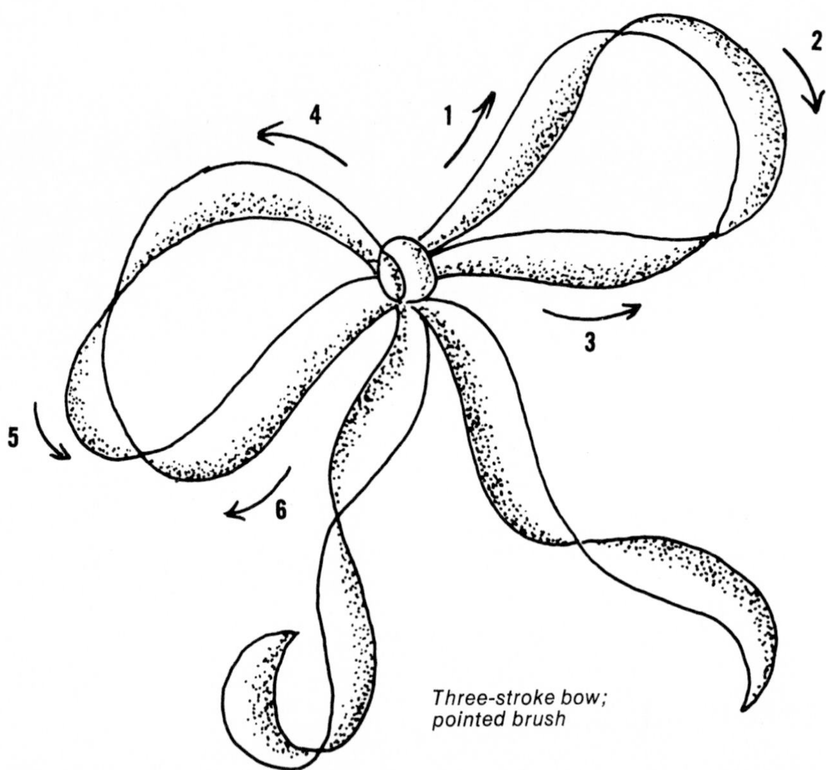

Three-stroke bow; pointed brush

Whenever you want to paint long, gracefully flowing ribbons, the pointed brush will give the best effect with the least effort. All bows and ribbons should be painted in two contrasting shades; they may also be triple-toned by adding white to one edge of the brush.

Before painting the lesson, place a square of tracing or waxed paper on your clipboard and review the basic comma stroke, using the flat brush. For practice, you may use any basic color you choose, making a dark and a light shade from it. Keep the paint consistency thin to ensure thin, tapering comma tails.

You will notice that the two-stroke bow is really just two curved and connected commas. The light shade is usually at the top of the bow (or outer edge of the brush) and the darker shade is below it (or to the inside of the brush). It is best to nearly fill the brush with the lighter shade first and then to stroke through the darker shade. When the darker shade is stroked into half of the brush first, it tends to overpower the lighter shade, resulting in the bow's being predominately dark with almost no light shading.

Start your bow with the flat brush (light shade to the outside of the brush, dark shade to the inside). Begin at the center to the right of the knot. Curve the stroke slightly up and down. As you begin the downcurve, slowly tip the flat brush to the inside and gradually lift the brush until only the inside corner paints a fine line, to complete the upper half of the bow.

The second stroke should have the light shade to the inside and the dark shade to the outside. Again, begin at the center knot but curve slightly down, around and up, and end in a fine line wrapped around the upper stroke, which completes the right side of the bow. The left side of the bow is painted in exactly the same manner. Keep your brush colors separated so that the bow will seem to turn. Remember to press the brush firmly to start the bow and to tip the inside corner slowly to finish the stroke. Sometimes you will want to paint this bow without a center or to use only a loop here and there to suggest a ribbon or bow peeking out from behind a flower arrangement.

To paint a knot, use the flat brush containing the light shade of paint and tip each corner in the dark shade. Press lightly just once to form the knot. This light touch produces a knot that is shaded from dark to light to dark. Sometimes you may want to use the corner of the brush to add a center line of dark color.

After you have stroked around the ribbon colors on three sides of your palette, use the spatula to clean up the areas beyond the pools of color. Stroking through used colors will dilute the shades on your brush so that the dark and the light shades will not be distinct from each other.

Now practice a few ribbons, using the flat brush. These can be just short suggestions of a ribbon or long flowing ones. As the ribbon ends, lift the brush and tip it on one corner to paint a fine tapering line. When you have finished practicing, clean the brush thoroughly and prepare to paint the lesson.

Brushes

Ribbon	Large pointed brush
Blossoms, leaves, and fill-in flowers	Small flat brush
Blossom centers and stems	Small pointed brush

Colors

Ribbon and bow

Darker shade	Titanium white mixed with a bit of alizaran crimson and a bit of Prussian blue (similar to swatch #5).
Lighter shade	Titanium white added to a small amount of the above color.

Blossoms

Blue-green	Titanium white mixed with a bit of viridian green to match swatch #12.
Yellow	Titanium white mixed with a bit of cadmium yellow medium to match swatch #20.
Dusky pink	A bit of Prussian blue added to darker ribbon color for a deeper shade.
Leaves	Titanium white mixed with permanent green light and a bit of burnt sienna.
Blossom centers	Leaf shade accented with titanium white.

Photograph #14

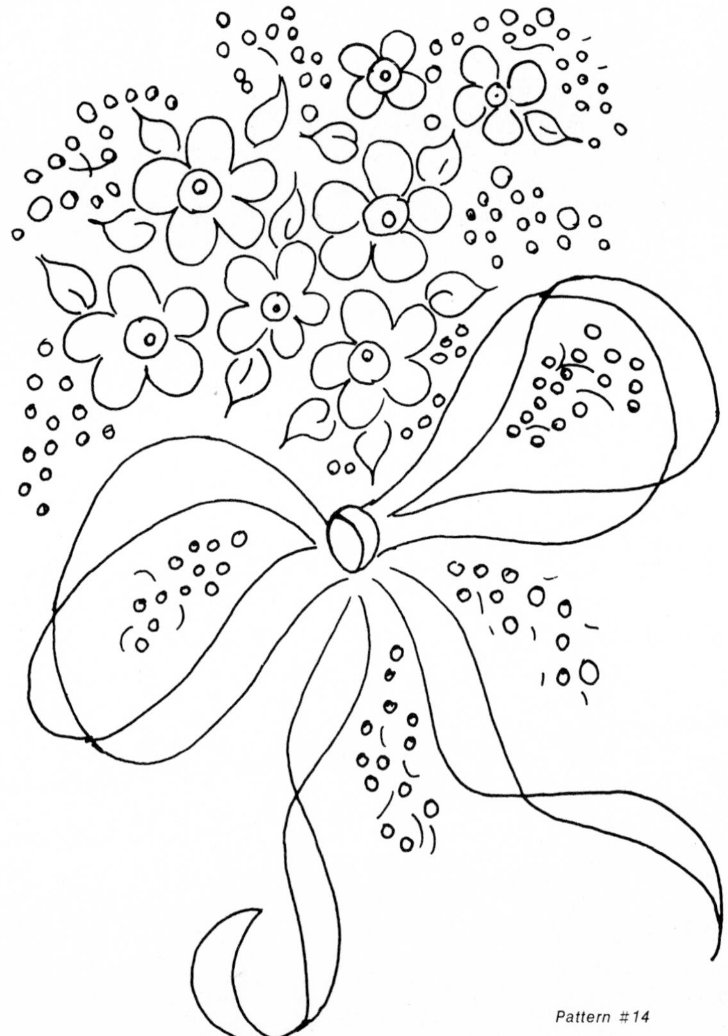

Pattern #14

Lesson Pattern

The color lesson of ribbons and bows is painted with the large pointed brush and uses three strokes for each side of the bow. This type of bow is wide and gives a flowing, turned effect.

Using the large pointed brush, half fill it with the lighter shade. Then stroke the opposite side into the deeper shade until the two colors blend on the palette. Keep the light shade to the outside of the brush and the dark shade to the inside.

Begin the first stroke at the center to the right of the knot. Lightly touch down the point of the brush and then press the bristles flat to fill the ribbon pattern, slowly lifting the brush so that the line comes to a fine point as the ribbon begins to turn.

Then turn the brush so that the dark shade is on the outside of the brush, and follow the curved area of the pattern. Again, press and lift as described above.

The third stroke begins at the center, with the lighter color inside and the darker color outside. Stroking in the same way, follow the pattern outline. Since this stroke also ends on a fine line, it will blend into the curve of the second stroke and the shading will give the effect of a turned ribbon. The opposite half of the bow is painted in the same manner.

To form the knot, use the flat brush filled with the light shade. Then tip each corner of the brush in the dark paint. Using just the tip, form a left- and a right-side comma. If necessary, add another light touch to the center of the knot.

The ribbon is painted just as the bow, turning the brush to reverse the color where the pattern indicates a turn in the ribbon.

Now that the ribbon and bow are painted, the rest of the lesson is up to you. You've had much practice painting blossoms, fill-in flowers, and leaves, so it should be easy.

LESSON 12

Rosebuds

You are going to learn to paint a rose by first learning to paint a shaded bud. In earlier lessons, you first painted large fruits and flowers in order to become accustomed to handling the brush and more experienced in painting with shaded strokes. Now you're ready to use those shaded strokes to paint something much smaller.

Look at the pattern. You will notice that there are three large and three smaller buds composing this design. The larger bud will be made using the small flat brush—just two shaded strokes will complete it. The smaller bud will also be painted with the small flat brush in just one or two strokes. In fact, you'll be using the small flat brush to paint the rose, the bud, the leaves, the ribbons and the fill-in flowers. The stems, veins, and tendrils are always painted with a small pointed brush.

Practice Rosebuds

Before painting this lesson design, slip some paper into your clipboard and practice the rosebud stroke for a few minutes. The colors used are alizaran crimson mixed with a bit of burnt sienna and a bit of titanium white. The shading color is white. (You may paint these in another shade if you prefer.) First, thin the red shade a little with a few drops of turpentine. The white may be a little thicker than the red shade but should still flow easily. (Sometimes the completed rosebud will have a tiny hole in its center. This can be avoided by first making a little center line or a small dot of red before starting the stroke. The stroke will hide this as it is completed, and the bud will appear completely closed in the center.) Stroke through the red shade until the brush is nearly full. Then turn the unfilled edge into the pool of white, stroking two or three times until you see a slight shading on your palette. There should also be a small white edge of paint on one side of the brush. Keep the white at the top of the brush, the darker red below it and toward the center.

Begin the upper stroke (as for the zinnia) in a comma stroke, painting from left to right. One comma stroke will fill in the upper half of the bud. Pick up more white so that you have an edge of white on the brush, and repeat the comma stroke, beginning again at the left side. This stroke will swing down, then up and slightly around the right side of the upper stroke. Now you have a pretty two-stroke rosebud.

ROSEBUD— open construction to show stroking

ROSEBUD— painted with one dot and two comma strokes

Remember to keep the colors on your brush in the same position for both strokes. The white is always at the top of the brush and the darker color is always below it on the opposite (or lower) side. Keeping your brush filled in this manner will enable you to paint the upper half of the bud in just one stroke. The darker shade will form the center and blend outward into the pink-edged-in-white. Keeping the brush and colors in the same position as you drop down to paint the lower half of the bud will automatically shade the bud from a darker base—up to the white curved edge accenting the bud center. As you practice this, you will notice that your rosebud can be either narrow or wide at the top, depending upon the amount of brush pressure you use. Remember the zinnia lesson, and use its curved-stroke technique to make these buds—curving upward even more to produce a long, slender bud.

Think of painting a small leaf as you paint the small pointed bud. Starting from the stem line, paint outward to a fine point. Fill the brush with color and edge one or both sides with white. This usually can be painted with one small stroke. Just press down on the brush lightly (don't move it) and then slowly lift it, tipping it to one corner as you lift so that the bristles still touching will end the stroke in a delicate point.

Put out a little more of the permanent green light and add a bit of white to your palette to paint a few tendrils around the buds. Add turpentine to the green until it is quite thin, as these lines should be very wispy and delicate. With the small pointed brush moistened with green, begin this stroke at the base of the bud, curving closely along the sides and beyond the bud to end in a slight curve. In green, paint a small oval at the base of the buds, accenting it with a contrasting shade of green or with white. Take a close look at color Photograph #15 and Pattern #15 for these details. Notice that sometimes the tendrils are painted slightly over each side of the bud and that they also creep up into the center area in a leaflike effect before they are extended into a fine line. Experiment with the technique: Press on the small pointed brush as though you were painting a leaf, and slowly lift the brush so that only the tip completes the line.

You have probably noticed that your brush is picking up the damp red color as you paint the green tendrils over the buds. Just wipe the brush in the tissue to remove the red color before picking up green for the next tendril. The green shade used over the buds should be dark enough to show a contrast and also dark enough not to show the slight bleeding of the red. The small amount of red paint that might remain in your brush won't change the shade of green you are using. In fact, you will often add red shades to green to get a variety of soft green shades. If there should be too much bleeding, spray the buds with a fixative and let dry before going on to the tendrils.

Brushes

Rosebuds, leaves, and ribbon	Small flat brush
Stems, tendrils, and veins	Small pointed brush

Colors

Rosebuds	Alizaran crimson mixed with a bit of burnt sienna and a bit of titanium white, thinned with turpentine.
Leaves	
Darker shade	Permanent green light mixed with cadmium yellow medium, a bit of burnt sienna, and a bit of titanium white.
Lighter shade	Titanium white added to some of the above color.

Stems, tendrils, and bud accents

Burnt sienna mixed with some of the darker leaf shade.

Ribbon

Viridian green mixed with titanium white to match swatch #11, shaded with titanium white or a contrasting shade of green.

Fill-in flowers

Painted as in previous lessons, using both green and white on the same corner of the brush.

Photograph #15

Pattern #15

Lesson Pattern

Mix paint and paint all the rosebuds. Spray on fixative when finished if necessary.

Next, paint the leaves, as you have done before, and then the stems, veins, tendrils, and bud accents.

The fill-in flowers and ribbon may be painted last. Here we have another perfect place for this useful little fill-in flower. It fills in areas that may look a little blank to you and also adds a graceful note to the design.

Practice the rosebud often, as its construction and one-stroke shading is important in the rose lesson to come.

Rosebuds and flowers on a folk-art cupboard. Courtesy Joyce W. Hundley, Dutch Village.

Photograph #16

LESSON 13

Plums

In this lesson on painting variously hued plums, you will be working with variations on the color cobalt violet. You can purchase this shade commercially or you can mix your own by using alizaran crimson, a bit of

Prussian blue, and a very small amount of white. Whatever your choice, the resulting shade will be a very bright color, one that can be varied in many ways. By adding a bit of alizaran crimson to it plus a bit of white, you can obtain a variety of redder shades. By further adding raw umber, you can deepen it to any intensity you like. You can even add a bit of Prussian blue for a deeper shade yet. Experiment with these shades, adding white, red, blue, or brown to the violet to find the ones you prefer.

Brushes

Fruit and leaves	Large flat brush
Blossoms	Small flat brush
Flower centers and fine detail	Small pointed brush

Colors

Blue plums	
Undercoat	Prussian blue mixed with titanium white to match swatch #8, thinned with turpentine as needed.
Deepen and shade	Cobalt violet mixed with a bit of alizaran crimson and a bit of raw umber, thinned with turpentine as needed.
Deeper accent	A bit of raw umber mixed with some of the above shade, thinned with turpentine as needed.
Green plum	
Undercoat	Lighter plum-leaf green.
Branches and twigs	Cadmium yellow medium mixed with a bit of burnt umber and titanium white to match swatch #45; burnt umber added to the darker leaf green (similar to swatch #38).
Darker accents	Burnt umber, shaded with a bit of titanium white.
Lighter accents	Titanium white.
Leaves	
Darker shade	Permanent green light mixed with cobalt violet and titanium white (similar to swatch #38).
Lighter shade	Titanium white added to some of the above shade to match swatch #39.
Stems and veins	A bit of raw umber added to deeper shade of leaf green.
Blossoms	Cobalt violet mixed with titanium white.
Blossom centers	Cadmium yellow medium mixed with white to match swatch #20, accented with titanium white and lighter shade of leaf green.

Pattern #16

Lesson Pattern

Blue Plums

After mixing the colors for the blue plum undercoat, transfer Pattern #16 to tracing paper and anchor it firmly to your clipboard. Study the pattern and notice that, again, there is an underneath plum that must be painted before the plum that extends over it.

Begin to paint the plum that's underneath, using the blue undercoat shade that has been thinned with a drop or two of turpentine. Remember to apply the undercoat just *inside* the fruit outline. Apply a heavy undercoat for fruit, but be certain that it does not stand in high ridges. Wipe the brush in the lap rag or tissue, and with one corner of the brush, pick up the deeper shading color. Begin to add this at the center top of the plum. As you near the base of the plum, the color will have weakened, so wipe the brush and pick up additional deeper color to continue around the base of the plum. If you turn the brush over, there will usually be enough color left to paint the lighter side of the plum. This will result in a slightly lighter shading.

You may wish to deepen this plum shade on the left even more than is shown in Photograph #16. In that case, pick up more of the shading color and apply it to the left side, diminishing as you approach the base of the plum. If you want to add the bulge line, use the technique you learned in the peach lesson. Before repeating the deeper shading color to form the bulge line, wipe your brush in the lap rag and dry-brush the shading color lightly into the blue so that a little of the undercoat shows through. Unless you wipe the color from the brush frequently, you will just be moving the paint around instead of shading. Do only a little dry-brushing because you will next add to the plum quite a lot of titanium white that has been thinned with a drop or two of turpentine. Pat the white on the center area of the plum; wipe the brush and lightly blend the white into the blue and purple. You may prefer to sponge this instead of dry-brushing. Either technique gives a pretty effect. Plums can stand a lot of additional white, so you may want to leave the paint quite heavy, patting it to give it a frosted appearance. Another little shading trick to try: As you dry-brush, pull the color across the plum slightly in several light strokes. Wipe the brush and either sponge or dry-brush in a circular motion to give the effect of roundness.

Now paint the upper plum just as you have the first one.

Green Plum

Mix the leaf-green shades, but do not add the white just yet. Lift aside a small amount of the lighter green and combine it with a little white, if desired, for the undercoating of the green plum. Complete the undercoating and then wipe the brush in the lap rag thoroughly. On one corner of the brush, pick up a bit of the green plum color and apply it very sparingly to the left side of the green plum, brushing across the bottom and up around the right side. Apply the bulge line if you choose, dry-brushing and blending for the effect you want. Add a little white highlight to the center of this plum if you wish.

Branches and Twigs

Branches can be quite complicated to paint, but this is a quick and easy way to begin. You can experiment further and add some shading tricks of your own.

Mix the two suggested colors. Thin with turpentine and fill the small flat brush with both colors. Paint down from the base of the plum and taper to a fine point at the end. Generally this two-shade effect looks very pretty just as it comes from the brush. For a little more contrast, accent the hollows and deeper areas of the ridges on the twigs with a bit of burnt umber, thinned with turpentine. You can also highlight the top of the branch by painting some white in, using short curved strokes with the small pointed brush. Apply the white in a series of two or three small comma strokes, then skip an area, and add a few more. These can be lightly blended by dry-brushing in a circular motion or they can be left just as they are if the effect is pleasing to you. On some backgrounds you will find it necessary for contrast to add the deeper shade to both sides of the branches. On other backgrounds you may want to add more white to give a silver birch or frosted look to the lighter side. Any of these methods gives a nice branch without much detailed work.

The upper branch is painted in the same way as the lower. Again, use the small pointed brush and very thin dark paint to paint in the oval at the end of the twig. Inside the oval, lightly brush in an off-white to suggest the hollow of the stem.

Leaves, Stems, and Veins

On the dark side of the leaves, two shades of green – the light and the dark – are used. With the two colors still in the brush, stroke into the edge of the white two or three times and paint in the opposite half of the leaf. You won't need to clean the brush right now; just squeeze it in the tissue to remove any excess paint and pick up more light and dark paint for the darker half of the next leaf. This not only saves time but also adds variety to the leaf shades. Paint the stems and leaf veins as you have before.

Blossoms

The blossoms will be painted with the press-stroke, as you have done before. The centers are accented with a bit of the lighter leaf-green shade and with white.

Photograph #17

LESSON 14

Violets

This lesson may surprise you. You are going to mix your own shades of blue and purple from your imagination and from looking at the color photograph. Because of the large variety of colors, you will need only very small amounts of paint for this lesson.

By using cobalt violet and adding to it a bit of alizaran crimson, you'll get a brighter violet, which you may prefer. By adding raw umber, you may deepen this shade to almost black purple, or you may add Prussian blue for a still different coloring. And finally, by adding white to any of these shades, you may lighten it to any degree you choose. These combinations also work with Prussian blue. By adding raw umber, you can deepen this as much as you choose. By also adding a bit of purple, you will get an entirely different shade of blue. And adding white to this color will give an even greater variety of shades. A very nice effect can be created by mixing blue and purple together on the palette as you stroke into them, blending until the two colors merge as one on the brush. Do not clean the brush in turpentine very often but simply wipe it clean in tissue or the lap rag and resume painting with either the blue or the purple. This technique will give a much softer blending to the violet shade. You now have quite a selection of colors to use, so take your choice.

Look at Photograph #17, and notice that there are three or four shades of violets used to add interest to the design. Feel free to change the shading in any way that is pleasing and interesting to you. Be careful to add Prussian blue to your colors in very tiny amounts, as it is a very strong color.

Brushes

Ribbon	Large pointed brush
Violets and leaves	Small flat brush
Flower centers, stems, and veins	Small pointed brush

Colors

Ribbon	Alizaran crimson mixed with a bit of raw umber and titanium white.
Leaves	Permanent green

	light mixed with a bit of either raw umber or the violet shade and titanium white. Lighten and shade with titanium white.
Violets	
Deep blue	Prussian blue or permanent green light mixed with a bit of raw umber and titanium white to produce desired shade.
Pale blue	Above shade mixed with more titanium white.
Purple	Cobalt violet mixed with a bit of Prussian blue, a bit of raw umber, and titanium white to produce desired shade.
Violet centers	Ivory black, a bit of cadmium yellow medium, and a bit of Grumbacher red.

Lesson Pattern

Ribbon

Throughout this lesson the consistency of the paint—for ribbon, violets, and leaves alike—must be quite thin so that it flows easily. Paint the underneath

Pattern #17

part of the ribbon first—that is the section under the bow extending down into the fluttering ends. This will be painted with the large pointed brush as you learned in the ribbon lesson. Fill it with your favorite shades of pink, adding a deeper shade to one side of the brush and stroking one or two times into the edge of the white for the third lighter shade. Reverse the brush to suggest a turned ribbon, as was taught in the ribbon lesson.

Floral cabinet panels wreathed with roses and violets. Courtesy Joyce W. Hundley, Dutch Village.

Leaves

As you prepare the paint for the leaves, keep the paint quite thin. This will not only give a much softer look to the composition but will dry much more quickly. By the time you have completed the leaves and mixed your violet shades, the leaves should be dry enough to paint the violets right over them.

To paint the leaves, use the small flat brush. Stroke the deeper shade of green down one side of the leaf. With the paint still in the brush, stroke into the edge of the white (which also is quite thin) and complete the opposite, lighter half of the leaf. The violet leaf is constructed just as all the other leaves are except that it is a little wider at the top. It can even be a little more rounded at the tip of the leaf if you prefer.

Violets and Buds

Before painting the violets, lay your pattern aside for a few moments and experiment with the various shades of blue and purple you have mixed so that you can decide which shade you prefer.

The violet will be painted very much like the daisy. Using the small flat brush, apply firm pressure as you start the stroke. Tip the brush to one corner as the petal is ended in the center area. As you add the petals to the violet, a very small hole in the center will appear that will be filled in later with a black V accent and a very small dot of both yellow and red. For a more delicate violet shading, experiment with this trick: First fill the brush with white, then stroke one edge into the purple shade—stroking until you see a slight blending on the palette (but not a definite stripe, which is most unattractive). Be sure to thoroughly blend the colors in your brush as you stroke through them on the palette. In this way, you will have a very pretty shaded effect without having a stripe.

To paint the buds and the little sprigs that extend below the leaves, use the *side* of the flat brush with blue and white or purple and white together on the brush. Apply light pressure to form the one-stroke leaf beside this spray of buds.

Violet Centers

Now you are ready to add the black V and the center dots of yellow and red. Thin the black with turpentine until it is very, very thin. This little V must be lightly and delicately painted in—using only the tip of the small pointed brush with a very light touch. Add more black to the tip of the brush to accent the little black whiskers on the violet petals. Finally, thin the red and the yellow with turpentine and add just a dot of each to the center. Next, add the final accent lines of green around the buds and the flowers. Be sure that the paint is very thin and that you use only the tip of the small pointed brush for this fine detail.

This pattern can be extended for use on a larger object by adding more violets beyond the ribbon and beyond the center leaves. You may surprise yourself by painting these violets without a pattern. They are really very simple to paint, and the only problem you may have is with the shading. To solve this problem, just remember to blend the colors together on the palette and in your brush before you paint.

OPTIONAL PATTERN

Violets and Rosebuds

The design on Pattern #18 is small enough to fit on many smaller objects or, for a larger object, it can be enlarged by adding more violets and more rosebuds. This lesson is painted in the same colors as was the previous violet lesson. Violets and rosebuds offer an especially pretty combination and are adaptable to decorating a variety of household and gift-giving items. This little nosegay is of an ideal size to fit on such objects as cannisters, small wastepaper baskets, or tissue boxes. Painted wood boxes for jewelry or trinkets also could be used for this design.

Photograph #18

The violet pattern used in this first lesson could be extended to a much larger size and used on a chest of drawers or the back of a small chair.

Leaves and Violets

Since many of the leaves are beneath violets, paint them first, using the small flat brush. Since one side of each leaf is deeper than the other, they will be painted, just as in the earlier violet lesson, by stroking

Pattern #18

into the deeper shade of thin, green paint and then stroking immediately into the white for a slightly lighter green for the opposite side of the leaf. After the leaves are completed, clean your brush and set it aside. Spray the leaves with a fixative and allow to dry before going on to the violets.

Use the same brush for the violets, painting them as you did in the previous lesson. To give a slightly pink shade to the blues and purples, add a bit more alizaran crimson, diluting it with some white. When finished, clean your brush in turpentine.

Rosebuds

Use the small flat brush again to paint the rosebuds, tendrils, and stems. The colors to mix for the rosebuds are alizaran crimson and a bit of raw umber, shaded with white. You may vary the rosebud shade in any way you choose by adding more or less white or brown. Paint rosebuds as you did in Lesson 12 and then spray them with a fixative and allow to dry before going on to the tendrils.

The stems and tendrils around the rosebud will be more effective if you first darken a small amount of permanent green light with a little of the rosebud red or a little raw umber. This is necessary because the green will pick up the red from the still-damp rosebud and dilute its shade slightly.

Photograph #19

LESSON 15

Trees

This lesson is practically mistake-proof! The only real brush stroke involved is the basic comma stroke, which is extended into a long, curved line and applied on the base of the trunk. The rest of the tree is sponged in—or stippled—with a dark green background. The leaf effect is painted over the still-wet background for an automatic shading.

Brushes

Tree, leaves, and bird body	Small flat brush
Bird eyes, beak, feet, and feathers	Small pointed brush

Colors

Tree trunk	Burnt umber mixed with burnt sienna and enough titanium white to match swatch #51; permanent green light mixed with burnt umber (similar to swatch #38).
Leaf background	Permanent green light mixed with a bit of ivory black.
Leaves	Permanent green light mixed with cadmium yellow medium to match swatch #40; permanent green light mixed with a bit of burnt umber (similar to swatch #38).
Bird body	Permanent green light mixed with titanium white

Pattern #19

	(similar to swatch #11); cadmium yellow medium mixed with titanium white to match swatch #19; a bit of burnt sienna added to some of the above shade (similar to swatch #59).
Wings	Cobalt violet mixed with a bit of titanium white. More white added for a lighter shade.
Feet and eye	Ivory black, thinned with turpentine.

Lesson Pattern

Tree Trunk

Using the small flat brush, fill the inside of the brush with brown and the outside with the green. At the top of the tree and to the inside of the tree trunk, begin the basic stroke. Press firmly and tip to one corner as you trail the point off in a slightly jagged edge at the base of the tree. Refilling the brush with the two colors, paint in the left stroke of the tree base. Next, paint a long comma at the upper right, suggesting a knothole. Turn the pattern upside-down to paint the second comma, which also suggests a knothole. Turn the pattern right side up again to apply the basic comma strokes to finish the base of the tree. Clean your brush in turpentine to use in the next step.

Leaf Background

Lightly stipple in the very dark green paint that will form the outline of the leaves. This should be done rather haphazardly—do not apply it too solidly. In fact, you can just dabble to your heart's content because there is no real painting involved in applying this background color.

Leaves

Clean the flat brush in turpentine and fill it with the two shades of leaf green. For these leaves, you will not really be making a leaf stroke but will use the *narrow* side of the brush to "pounce" in a suggested leaf. Think of the shape of a sheaf of wheat as you paint these leaves, spraying out in groups of three and five. Begin at the base of the tree center where the green paint is a little heavier, and pounce the brush in about three pounces, one to the right, one to the left, and one in the center. Between these, extending out like a sheaf of wheat, add two more pounces with the side of the brush. The wet background color and the two shades of green on your brush will do all the shading work for you. Be sure to make this tree fluffy on all sides. Let the areas be detached somewhat so that the shape resembles the shape of a shamrock or a clover leaf, for a more open look. As you finish, dangle a few leaves in a detached manner to soften the effect. Here, you may want to sprinkle a few leaves at the base of the tree. The leaves could also use additional yellow or white to give a varied effect. Experiment to see what suits you.

Bird

You learned how to paint birds in Lesson 6. Using the suggested colors, refresh your memory by practicing again. Then add to your finished tree painting, using the suggested colors.

LESSON 16

Cherries

In past lessons you have learned to paint and shade two red fruits. The apple lesson was shaded in bright red, and the strawberry lesson was shaded in an orange-red. In the cherry lesson you will add another range of colors to your repertoire—the pink-to-wine range. This color combination adapts well to nearly any color background. However, always feel free to change colors to suit your purpose. You may prefer bright red cherries, the colors used in the strawberry lesson, or the red shade that trims your kitchen. You'll learn to paint a turned leaf in this lesson. As you look at Pattern #20 and Photograph #20, look for possibilities for using a grouping of only three cherries for smaller objects. You may use the small flat brush instead of the large to paint smaller cherries and groupings.

Brushes

Cherries	Large flat brush
Stems and veins	Small pointed brush
Leaves	Large pointed or large flat brush

Colors

Cherries	
Undercoat	Grumbacher red mixed with titanium white (slightly deeper than swatch #3), thinned with turpentine.
Deepen and shade	Grumbacher red

Pattern #20

	mixed with alizaran crimson and a bit of raw umber for a bright wine shade.
Darker accent	Raw umber added to a bit of the above shade for a deep wine shade.
Lighten and highlight	Titanium white, thinned with turpentine.
Leaves	
Darker shade	Permanent green light mixed with a bit of Grumbacher red and titanium white to match swatch #38. Titanium white for turned leaf shading.
Lighter shade	Cadmium yellow medium mixed with titanium white.
Stems and veins	A bit of raw umber added to some of the above darker green shade.

Lesson Pattern Cherries

First, undercoat the cherries that lie beneath other cherries. Beginning at the top of the pattern, undercoat the first cherry in the pink undercoat shade. Complete this entire shading before painting the overlapping cherry in the middle and the one at the top. Proceed down the pattern, each time choosing the

Photograph #20

underneath cherry to shade and complete before going on to add the overlapping cherry. Thin the undercoat shade with a few drops of turpentine so that it spreads easily and leaves no high ridges. Apply the undercoat just inside the cherry outline so that the brighter wine shade can later be painted just beyond it to accent and catch in the undercoat shade smoothly. The shading color should be sparingly applied to the outer edge. Add only a small amount of this color to one corner of your brush.

To paint the bulge lines in the cherries, proceed—as in the previous lessons—to dry-brush lightly so that a small amount of the pink undercoat is showing before the deeper shade is applied to form the bulge. Again, dry-brush and blend for a lighter color in the center of the cherry. If you prefer, you may darken the cherries that are underneath more than those lying on top—where they would normally catch more light. You may prefer to shade more of the cherries with the very deep wine shade. Varying the shading in the cherries adds interest and makes a prettier composition.

When you have completed painting all the cherries, add a white highlight where you imagine the light would strike the cherry. You will notice that a small comma of dark green is painted on the cherry at the base of the stem. This can be added as you paint the stems and leaves.

Leaves

The leaves in this lesson can be painted with either the large pointed brush or the large flat brush. When using the flat brush, remember to use the corner of the flat brush as you would use the tip of the pointed brush. This is the reason you should keep your flat brushes thoroughly cleaned and reshaped. A bulging, fuzzy-edged flat brush will not paint neat designs.

The unturned leaves in this lesson are constructed just as the basic leaf. One side is darker than the other side. Paint in the darker green first, and then, with this color in the brush, stroke into the edge of pale yellow two or three times and complete the other half of the leaf. Go ahead and paint all the unturned basic leaves now.

If you need practice painting the turned leaf, put your pattern aside and review. Perhaps you should try this leaf using the pointed brush and then try it with the large flat brush to see which is easier to use. Generally, the turned leaf is made more easily with the pointed brush, but you may do equally as well with the flat brush. Fill the pointed brush with the darker green paint, stroking into the edge of pale yellow to give a slightly lighter shading on the lighter half of the leaf.

Gently wipe the brush in the tissue, and refill it with the deeper shade to complete the darker half of the leaf. Stroke into the edge of white two or three times, leaving a small edge of white on the side of the brush. With the dark green on the brush, lay it along the side of the leaf with the white extending toward the center, and paint two or three small scallops down the curve of the leaf, tapering to an end. It isn't necessary to scallop these several times—sometimes just one long curve will produce a very effectively turned leaf. Remember to flatten the pointed brush very thoroughly as you stroke into the paint. Painting a turned leaf is somewhat like painting the ribbon in that you apply heavy-to-light pressure to get the turned effect.

Now, pick up your pattern and finish the turned leaves. If you are making them really well, paint more than the pattern indicates. You can make turned leaves from any leaf pattern by using this technique, always making sure that the light-against-dark contrast will show. The turned part of the leaf is usually the lighter.

Stems and Veins

When the leaves are all completed, add the dark green for the stems and the vein effect. Be sure to thin the dark green quite a bit by adding a few drops of turpentine. Using only the tip of the small pointed brush, lightly paint in the vein effect. Never try to use a dark brown for the vein effect. This produces a rather harsh appearance and attracts more attention to this detail than to the fruit.

Cherries can be used alone for a very effective decoration, or you may prefer to combine them with other fruit on a wood panel. A matching panel could be decorated with a spray of strawberries, using the same shading colors. If these are to be hung in pairs, vary the arrangement somewhat by planning a third panel of smaller size decorated with fruit of another color.

The background color possibilities for this lesson, as in the other red-fruit lessons, are numerous. Any color looks well on off-white or on ivory, but a soft gray-green is also a very lovely shade. And, strangely enough, red-on-red can be a very striking combination. Later, as you take up antiquing and various color effects, you will find that an antiqued red object that is decorated with red fruit and a few blossoms or daisies in an off-white is a very striking combination.

Photograph #21

LESSON 17

Painting Fruit for Effect

In this lesson you will paint and shade fruit combinations using only white and two shades of brown—raw umber and burnt sienna—for shading. Rather than being realistic, this lesson demonstrates the effectiveness of objects painted with unusual colors and combinations. After you have finished this lesson, you may paint with any other color you choose.

Brushes

Fruit and leaves	Large flat brush
Branch	Small flat brush
Stems, veins, and curliques	Small pointed brush

Colors

Cherries	Raw umber shaded with titanium white.
Leaves	Raw umber shaded with titanium white.
Apple	Raw umber mixed with burnt sienna shaded with titanium white.
Stems, veins, and curliques	Raw umber, thinned with turpentine.

Lesson Pattern

Cherries

Look at the pattern and choose the point at which you think you should begin. As before, you

Pattern #21

should have chosen the fruit that is underneath, and you should complete it before painting the overlapping fruit. In this pattern, the cherry that is lying under the leaves on the lower right part of Pattern #21 is the best starting point.

Then, prepare the paint. Add a drop or two of turpentine to each of the brown shades, and place a small amount of titanium white on the palette for shading. Using the large flat brush, fill the hollow of the cherry with white. Lightly wipe the brush in the tissue, and with one corner of it, begin to shade the left side of the cherry, continuing all around it, with raw umber. Lightly wipe the paint from the brush and begin to blend the white into the brown, using a pivoting or circular motion. Use the white generously and watch the shading effect that appears as you dry-brush these colors together. As is true of all the fruit you paint, one side should be darker than the other. Look at Photograph #21 and notice that the raw umber is also quite pronounced on the lower portion of the cherry. For a little more contrast, you may dry-brush a very little bit of burnt sienna across the top of the cherry. Add a small white highlight.

Proceed to the cluster at the right side of the apple, beginning with the cherry that is underneath the others. Since only half of this cherry is showing, this is all you need to paint. Apply the white just as before. Gently wipe the brush in tissue before adding the raw umber to one corner of the brush. Shade lightly, dry-brushing for a blended effect. Complete each cherry shading before starting the next one above it. After these are completed, paint the two cherries to the left of the apple in the same manner. Add white highlights to each, and on some, dot in a few black speckles with the tip of the small pointed brush.

Leaves and Apple

Still using the large flat brush, paint the three leaves to the outside of the apple now, using your newly learned turned leaf technique. Wipe your brush.

Next, paint the apple just as you did the cherries, filling the center of the apple first with white. Lightly squeeze the brush in the tissue, and on one corner, add the raw umber. On the opposite corner, add the burnt sienna. Begin at the center top of the apple to blend these two colors into the white. You may need to pick up more of the brown shades on each corner of the brush in order to completely encircle the apple. Then begin to dry-brush and blend, making sure to wipe the brush frequently in the tissue or lap rag. When this is completed to your satisfaction, add a white highlight to the center of the apple.

Branch, Stems, Veins, and Curliques

You may now add the stems to the cherries, using raw umber. Give a little more depth to the area around the stem by adding a bit more of this color. Do the same to the apple, painting in a V to indicate where the stem is attached to the base of the apple. Shade the stem with raw umber and a little white.

Use raw umber, softened in turpentine, with white to paint the branch. When it is completed, dry-brush a bit of burnt sienna across it for a little added shading. You may also want to add additional white for the lighter side of the branch. Lightly spot the branch with black or raw umber, softened with turpentine – use just the tip of the small pointed brush to do this.

Paint the veining in the leaves, using the raw umber softened in turpentine. Then go on to finish the painting by painting in all the curliques.

You might want to look through your swatch chart, select some other colors, and try this "effect" painting for another composition.

Combination fruit arrangements painted for effect. Painted oak and gumwood, eighteenth century, N.Y. The Metropolitan Museum of Art, Rogers Fund, 1909.

Photograph #22

LESSON 18

Folk Art

The twentieth-century's contribution to folk art is its new shading techniques. No longer are homes decorated in the dull, earthy colors of the past but rather in softer blendings and brighter colors. By using the blended brush stroke for your painting, you'll be able to use the traditional folk designs but change them completely by your choice of color.

Pattern #22 can be painted quickly with the shaded brush strokes. By filling the brush with two or three colors at a time, you can create, with one shaded stroke, the same effect that was created in the past over several days' drying time. Not only that, but by your choice of color, you can change this pattern to fit any color scheme. You may use the earthy, dark colors that are traditional or you may prefer bright reds, brilliant greens, blues, and yellows for a more modern effect.

The shadings in this lesson are soft and will easily fit with many pastel interiors. By changing the colors, this pattern could just as easily be made to look Oriental. Indeed, all our twentieth-century designers are influenced directly or indirectly by other cultures. No folk art is pure. Even our own is not truly ours in origin. It was influenced by the other countries of the world and by the people who brought it to America, changing it and adapting its designs to suit their needs and the materials they were able to use. You, too, can change these designs to fit your home, its color scheme, and your tastes. But you have an advantage over folk-art practitioners of the past in that the development of the shaded brush-stroke technique and good paints and brushes enable you to finish your design days (or weeks) faster than your predecessors.

The colors in your swatch chart are a good example of the color range you have to choose from to decorate an object. After painting this lesson, you will probably come up with ideas of your own to incorporate. Consider the room you intend to use the object in, its coloring, and so on, and change the colors of this lesson accordingly. There are no rules to observe in folk art. So, first begin with this lesson and then let your imagination guide you to variations in color and style until you have created something entirely your own. To start you off on your own, you will not be given detailed instructions in this lesson for mixing colors. Use your small flat brush for the entire design. The large

Pattern #22

pointed brush, however, may also be used if you find that you are more comfortable using it.

Lesson Pattern

Corner Flowers

Begin the lesson by first painting the flowers at the upper right and lower left of Pattern #22. Using Photograph #22 as a guide, mix three shades to your liking—wine, deep pink, and pale pink. Place some titanium white on your palette. Fill the brush with pale pink and then stroke into the edge of the white until a

Folk-art coffee pot painted with basic comma strokes. By Marg Pond.

small edge of white appears on the brush. Paint the upper right flower center—the pink to the inside of the brush and the white to the outside—with two strokes. Turn the white edge of the brush to the opposite side on the second stroke. Pick up more of the pink shade, stroke into the white two or three times, and paint the top petal close to the center. The pink should be to the inside and the white to the outside. Repeat on the opposite side of the flower.

Wipe your brush in the tissue, fill it with the deeper shade of pink, and again stroke into the edge of the white two or three times. Apply the brush to the middle petal on each side of the flower.

Squeeze the brush in the tissue and then pick up the deep wine shade, again stroking into the white for a slightly shaded stroke. Apply the bottom petals on the flower just as you have the above two petals, painting from the outside in. With the deep wine shade still in the brush, pick up an edge of white. Keeping it to the outside, paint the bud of the flower. Reverse the brush so that the white is on the opposite side, and complete the bud with two shaded strokes.

Repeat this procedure to paint the flower at the lower left of the pattern.

Unicorn chest with detailed folk-art designs. Pennsylvania yellow pine and poplar (whitewood), ca. 1780.
The Metropolitan Museum of Art, Rogers Fund, 1909.

Center Flowers

Both center flowers are painted in the above manner, as well. Always begin the stroke at the large, or fat, part of the pattern, gradually tipping the brush to the side so that you end the stroke using just a few hairs of the corner. The flat brush works just as effectively as the pointed brush for this design. Remember to keep the paint thin enough to flow easily as you lightly press the stroke.

This design can be even more pastel if you stroke into the white more heavily. In fact, the amount of white used for shading will determine the finished effect. When these flowers have been painted, clean the brush.

Stems and Leaves

Mix two shades of green—one light and one olive—and thin both considerably so that they will flow easily enough to paint the stems. Fill the brush with the lighter green and the olive green. Using the side of the brush, begin the stroke at the base of the bud. Then, tip the brush flat as you curve, and again tip to one corner as you end the stroke. Stroke the winding stem throughout the pattern in the same manner.

To paint the leaves, again fill the brush with the lighter green and then the deeper green. Keeping the dark to the outside, begin the leaf stroke at the stem area and paint in a series of graduated commas until you have reached the point of the leaf. With the two colors still on your brush, stroke into the white two or three times and paint the other half of the leaf beginning at the upper part of the stem and, again, stroking in a series of four or five graduated, curved commas. These shades will blend together so that the finished effect will be shaded from light to dark. If you wish, squeeze the paint from the brush and lightly whisk the center of the leaf area to blend it slightly. Then add a thin accent line of darker green to suggest a stem.

LESSON 19

Crab Apples

Throughout the various red-fruit lessons, you have painted several different color combinations, each of which gave a different effect. The crab apples in this lesson will be shaded and streaked with several additional colors. (It's monotonous to paint red fruit always in the same shades, so be imaginative—mix and interchange the shadings. Use the colors of the strawberry lesson on apples or the cherry shades on strawberries. Let your choice of colors guide you to a variety of shading in all you paint.) The shading and streaked effect can also be applied to larger apples. You might want to add dark red streaks to green apples or strawberries, brown streaks to dark yellow or green apples, or a few thin white streaks to other red fruit.

You'll be using a spray fixative in this lesson before painting the streaks. They are easier to add if the fruit color is only slightly tacky or completely dry, and the red shades are slower to dry than the other colors.

Brushes

Fruit and leaves	Large flat brush
Branches	Small flat brush
All fine detail	Small pointed brush

Colors

Crab apples	
Undercoat	Grumbacher red mixed with a bit of titanium white to match swatch #1.
Deepen and shade	Alizaran crimson mixed with Prussian blue, thinned with turpentine.

Whiskers	Grumbacher red mixed with a bit of Prussian blue.
Branches	Permanent green light mixed with a bit of Grumbacher red and enough titanium white to match swatch #38, mixed with more titanium white for a soft brown shade.
Leaves	Cadmium yellow medium mixed with permanent green light and enough titanium white to match swatch #42.
Streaks	Cadmium yellow medium, thinned slightly with turpentine.

Lesson Pattern

Crab Apples

When your colors are mixed, begin by undercoating the underneath crab apple to the left of Pattern #23. Then, undercoat the others.

Lightly wipe the brush in the tissue before adding a small amount of the deepen-and-shade color to one corner of the flat brush. Beginning at the center top of the left apple, start to shade the apple, deepening the left side more than the right side. Dry-brush and blend these colors, frequently wiping the brush in your lap rag. Add a small amount of the pale yellow shade to slightly lighten the center of the crab apple. Then shade the crab apple to the right. Next paint the top apple, and last add the lower apple.

When painting a cluster of fruit, you need to paint a slightly deeper shade to separate the overlapping fruit. Dry-brushing this additional color will give the

Photograph #23

sought-after shadow effect. Making sure that your brush has a little of the deeper red shade in it, tip one corner of it into the Prussian blue, which has been slightly thinned with turpentine. (Remember that this is a very strong color, so that you will need only a very small amount.) Lightly blend this deeper shade into the curved, darker side of the crab apple and lightly dry-brush. When painting the darker side of any fruit, feel free to add a bit more of the brown or blue (whichever you are using in your shading color) to further accent.

Now that the crab-apple shading is completed, add the finishing detail. Use the small pointed brush to

paint the fine black line and whiskers at the base of the apples. Mix a bit of Prussian blue and Grumbacher red for an almost black shade. Thin this color with a drop or two of turpentine, and use just the tip of the brush to paint the fine whiskers.

Branches and Leaves

The upper and lower branches are both painted outward from the base of the fruit. Use the small flat brush filled with both the green and brown shades. These colors should be thin enough to blend together as they are painted along the outline of the knobby branch. Use the small pointed brush with thin paint to add deeper accents along the darker side of the branch and a few curved lines across the top of them. You may prefer to lighten the top of the branches: If so, apply thin white paint in short curved strokes and lightly dry-brush. If it is easier for you, use the corner of the small flat brush to paint the curved highlights.

Paint all the leaves with the large flat brush. Two strokes are necessary to complete each half of the large leaves. Begin by painting all the underneath leaves, first painting the darker side. With this color still in your brush, stroke into the pale yellow shade once or twice to complete the lighter side of each leaf. If the outline of the crab apple shows through the two overlying leaves, add a stroke of darker green to this area to cover it.

The leaf veins are lightly painted with very thin green-brown paint. Adding a little brown to the deeper leaf green usually produces a grayed shade that will both contrast and blend. Avoid using a dark brown for leaf veins unless the leaf color is a shade of brown. The center vein should not run completly to the end of each leaf but should blend into it at a point about half or three-fourths of the leaf length.

By now you have probably discovered your own favorite shades of leaf greens. Feel free to substitute for the suggested leaf colors those that may be more pleasing to you. A variety of green shades can be made by mixing permanent green light and viridian green, adding brown or white for additional shades. Or you may prefer to mix your own shades of green using cadmium yellow medium and Prussian blue, with brown to deepen and white to lighten. For still more variety, add a little of the fruit or flower color to the green shades. Everyone sees colors differently, and by experiments with mixing them, you'll find shades that are especially pleasing.

Streaks

There is a little knack to learning just how lightly the brush must be used to give a streaking effect, and it's much easier to learn if the color to be streaked is almost or completely dry. If the streaks are added to a freshly painted color and if too much pressure is used on the brush, the colors will often blend instead of streak. Then, too, on a dry color, you can remove any unpleasing effects with a damp brush. So, use your spray fixative here, making sure it's dry before you continue.

To streak the crab apples you will need only a small amount of thin, bright yellow paint on one corner of the brush. The brush technique requires no pressure but a series of feathery, light whisks instead. If you want wider streaks, pick up more paint along the side of the brush. Experiment a little to get just the effect you want. If you should happen to have a small-bristle brush, you may find that its harsh hairs will skip and streak the thin paint very easily. Or you might try to add the streaks by using the stippling technique described in previous lessons.

Photograph #24

LESSON 20

Pineapples and Pine Cones

The pineapple, which has always been a symbol of hospitality, was used extensively to decorate chair backs and various other pieces of furniture during the colonial period. You may prefer to paint these pineapples in shadings other than the ones suggested—a color similar to swatch #47 is effective. The cross-hatch lines can be of brown, as in this lesson, and accented with green or almost any other color you choose. Here the pineapple is combined with pine cones, but it is frequently used with arrangements of other fruit in large or smaller designs. The addition of a pineapple to various fruit or vegetable arrangements can be very effective. Try it on your kitchen cabinets, trays, bread boards, or various boxes.

Brushes

Pineapple undercoat and shading and pine cones	Large flat brush
Pineapple lines and pine-cone needles	Small pointed brush
Pineapple leaves	Large pointed brush

Colors

Pineapple	
Undercoat	Cadmium yellow medium mixed with titanium white to match swatch #19.
Shading	Cadmium yellow medium mixed with cadmium red light and titanium white to match swatch #55.
Cross lines	Burnt umber mixed with burnt sienna and a bit of white to match swatch #52.
V in center of pineapple squares	Darker leaf green.
Leaves	
Darker shade	Permanent green light mixed with burnt umber and titanium white to match swatch #37.
Lighter shade	Cadmium yellow medium mixed with titanium white to match swatch #21.
Pine cones	Burnt umber mixed with burnt sienna and titanium white to match swatch #51; burnt umber thinned with turpentine; permanent green light mixed with a bit of Grumbacher red and enough titanium white to match swatch #38; cadmium yellow medium mixed with cadmium red light, viridian green, and enough titanium white to match swatch #47.
Pine-cone needles	Above shades of brown, green, and yellow-brown, thinned with turpentine.

Lesson Pattern

Pineapple

To begin, mix the pineapple paints. Using the

large flat brush, undercoat the entire pineapple in the yellow shade, blending as you have done previously with other fruit. After this is completed, clean the brush thoroughly and fill with the shading color. Beginning at the center top, use the entire width of the large flat brush to stroke around the entire pineapple. You will probably need to pick up this color several times as it is applied over the wet undercoat color. When this is completed, wipe the brush in the lap rag or the tissue and use it to blend the orange-red shade into the yellow background, stroking the brush in a circular motion. You may leave the center distinctly yellow if you prefer.

Add a few drops of turpentine to the brown shade. Using the small pointed brush, pick up the brown and lightly apply the cross-hatch lines of the pineapple, blending them in a slight curve. When this is completed, use the green shade of the leaves and the small pointed brush to paint in a small V in the center of the pineapple. Add a small spot of the orange shade just above the V and blend slightly.

This pineapple could be made to look quite modern by using colors other than these you would generally associate with a pineapple. In this case, the cross-hatch lines could be very firm, perhaps painted in black or a sharply contrasting color. They could be accented in the center area with a third color shaping the V, or a small comma could be used.

Leaves

Paint the pineapple leaves with the large pointed brush, using the green and yellow shades for one added stroke. Begin painting the two large center leaves at the back of the pineapple, painting from the base outward and ending in a point. Add more paint to complete the other leaves, following the same instructions. Last, add the small shaded leaf in the center.

Pine Cones

Before painting the pine cones, place your hand on the table, palm down, and notice its general shape.

Pattern #24

The receding rows of cones will generally resemble the way in which each finger is shorter than the last.

First paint the darker pine cone in the center of the pattern, using the large flat brush with green shade #38 and brown shade #47. Add a few drops of turpentine to these colors to help them flow easily.

Stroke into the edge of the green shade until you have filled about half the brush. Turn the unfilled half of the brush into the edge of the brown and stroke until this half is filled. Keep the brown shade to the outside of the brush and the green shade to the inside as you paint.

Use the press-stroke along with a small upward slide to form the pine cones. Begin by painting the first row at the lower center of the cone, press-sliding up to the center top. Paint the second row on either side of the center row, placing the first stroke a little short of the first row, as are your fingers. Complete one half of the cone and resume painting the opposite half in the same manner. You won't need to clean your brush until the pine cone is completed.

Before adding the accents to the cone, add a drop or two of turpentine to the white to thin it slightly. Slide the wide edge of the brush into the white, picking up only a bit along the edge. Lightly press the white edge over the end of each stroke to form the cone tips. You will probably need to pick up the white frequently since you are applying it sparingly.

Next paint the two lighter pine cones at each side of the pineapple, using two shades of brown (#51 and burnt umber, softened in turpentine) and yellow (shade #47). Paint them in the same manner as before, keeping the darker brown to the inside of the brush and the lighter brown to the outside. When the darker side of the cone is completed, lightly wipe the brush on the tissue or lap rag before adding the lighter brown and yellow shade to the other side. (The secret of blending these shades from dark to light is in not cleaning the brush in turpentine. Instead, lightly whisk the paint-filled brush over the tissue or lap rag and stroke into the brown and then the yellow shade.) Resume the press-stroke at the bottom of the cone, placing the brush at an outside angle and painting from the outside in. When this row is completed, lightly wipe the brush on a tissue and again stroke into the brown and yellow. Then paint the next-shorter row. You won't need to clean the brush in turpentine until the entire pine cone is completed. Add the white tips while the pine cone is still damp.

Needles

When you are completely finished, add the needles and fine lines around the pineapple leaves and pine cones. Use a small pointed brush and paint thinned with turpentine so that you can draw thin wispy lines.

After painting a few pine cones in various shadings, you can decide which colors you prefer. By using two shades of brown, you will have a darker pine cone. By adding the yellow shade, the cone will become a warmer shade of brown. And by adding a bit of green to the lighter side, a still different shading will appear. Try painting these without a pattern, now.

Begin at the lower center of the cone and press-stroke four, five, or six strokes up the center of the cone. Start at the base of the cone for the second row and stroke from the outside into the center row, angling the brush to the side as you stroke. Imagine stairsteps, and start each row at a slight side angle and a little shorter than the one you have completed.

You can add a few holly leaves and berries to your pine cones to make an entirely different and very attractive decoration for the holiday season.

Photograph #25

LESSON 21

Harlequin

No one is quite sure where the harlequin originated. The most popular explanation is that he evolved from a leading character found in the bawdy slapstick skits and farces of the old Roman mimes. His costume was a mass of patches, he wore a mask, and he carried a swatboard that had magical powers. In French vaudeville theater, *arlequin,* who is endowed with the grace and agility of a cat, plays a silent role of pantomime and wears a half-mask. The English harlequin was a lover and a magician. To compensate for his loss of speech, he was given a magic wand with which to protect his mistress from Clown and Pantaloon, who pursue her.

In this lesson you will practice two real timesavers. The first is using pen and ink to draw in fine detail; the second is letting the background do part of the work for you. Because you can't do pen work on an oily surface, put away the waxed paper and use your tracing paper for this lesson. You'll need an India ink pen with a #107 point and a bottle of black, waterproof ink. Wash the pen in soap and water to remove the oily film it will have picked up during handling. Take a few light practice strokes to get the feel of the point. Remember that you want only a small amount of ink on the point, so get in the habit of wiping it twice on the inner lip of the bottle before starting to draw. A large amount of ink on the point will sometimes run out in a blob. Since the #107 point is firm, it will require very little pressure to draw a line of constant thickness.

Start the penwork by outlining the black area that will be the harlequin's hair. Don't fill the hair area with ink—just outline it. Next, outline the mask and eye slits. Draw in the nose and mouth, the right ear, the cheek line, and the V in the neck. Outline the collar, and then draw the short black line on his right shoulder. Now, outline the belt and slippers. Let all the ink dry before going on.

Brushes

Entire figure	Small flat brush
Sharp details	Small pointed brush

Colors

Flesh tones	
Light	Burnt sienna mixed

Pattern #25

	with enough titanium white to match swatch #60.
Dark	Burnt sienna mixed with enough titanium white to match swatch #59.
Striped clothing	Permanent green light mixed with a bit of Grumbacher red and enough titanium white to match swatch #38.
Blue clothing	
Undercoat	Prussian blue mixed with enough titanium white to match swatch #8.
Deepen and shade	Prussian blue mixed with enough titanium white to match swatch #7.
Lighten	Titanium white.
Hair, mask, belt, and slippers	Ivory black.

Lesson Pattern

Flesh Tones

Mix a small amount of each of the two flesh tones. Paint the light flesh tones in the right side of the face, making sure that the paint meets the black lines (it won't matter if you go slightly over the lines). Fill in the darker flesh tone on the left side of the face. Squeeze the brush in the lap rag, and lightly blend together the two flesh tones where they join. If you have partially obscured the black lines in the face, you have a choice of ways to correct the defect: Either you can run the small end of a toothpick over the black lines, cleaning off the flesh paint, or you can wait until the painting is completely dry and retrace the black lines with ink. Go on to the other flesh areas, finishing the shading in each before moving on to the next. This is a good time to give your painting a light spray of fixative so that you won't smear it while working on the other colors.

Clothing

Next, paint the stripes. Since they won't be shaded, use your small flat brush to paint them in. If you haven't learned to control the width of your stroke, paint the stripes in two strokings—one on either edge of the stripe—using the side of your brush and lightly blending any ridge that may result where the strokes overlap. Put a drop or two of turpentine on the green paint on the palette to keep it moist while you go on to paint the blue sections. You will need the green later for the hat, cuff, and ribbon. Again, spray on a bit of fixative to prevent smearing.

Paint the blue parts of the harlequin costume in just the same way you painted the fruit. Starting with the shirt, undercoat one section at a time with blue shade #8. Wipe your brush in the lap rag and pick up a little of the darker blue. Stroke the blue under the left armpit and down the left side. Wipe your brush and blend the darker tone into the lighter undercoat. Now pick up a dab of white and paint a slightly lighter area on the top of the left shoulder and part of the way down the front of the shirt. Blend the white into the undercoat. Repeat the same series of steps on the half-sleeve on the left arm, deepening the blue under the arm and lightening it on top. Move on to the right leg, using Photograph #25 as a guide to shading. Spray with more fixative.

Use the green paint to finish up the ribbons, hat, and leg ruffle, using for the ribbons either the small flat brush or the large pointed brush. Moisten a bit of ivory black with turpentine, and fill in the black sections you first outlined in ink, using the small pointed brush.

There is an absence of paint in several areas of the figure. You have let the background carry part of the design. It matters little whether the background is white or a color—the design will look just as interesting either way.

LESSON 22

Berries and Dewdrops

Before you start to paint the berries in this lesson, mix all the colors needed. Then, on a sheet of tracing paper, paint a 1-inch-square swatch for each color. Add enough turpentine to the paint so that the swatches will be dry by the end of this lesson.

You will use these swatches to practice painting dewdrops after completing the lesson. They will be more easily painted if the undercoat is completely dry so that you can erase any mistakes without disturbing the background color. This lesson will make you a proficient dewdrop painter, since every little circlet painted on the berries is really a small dewdrop. You may even want to go back to fruit you have painted earlier and add to them a few dewdrops here and there.

The berries and leaves in this lesson are all painted with the small flat brush. The small pointed brush will be used to form the outline of the berries, the leaf accents, and the curliques around the berries. As you mix your shades of violet and red-violet, add enough turpentine to make a thin paint.

Each of these berries is painted or accented in two shades. They are all undercoated with a light and a deeper shade, which are slightly dry-brushed together for a shaded contrast before the tiny white circles are painted on.

Since some of the berries are under the leaves, Pattern #26 shows only part of the berries. Consequently, it is best to avoid the leaf area as much as possible. If you should happen to paint some of the berry inside the leaf outline, the leaf shades won't be affected because the berry colors should be almost dry by the time the leaves are added. Any remaining trace of the berry coloring will blend into the green leaves, making them even more attractive.

Brushes

Berries and leaves	Small flat brush
Berry detail, stems, and vine effect	Small pointed brush

Colors

Berries	
Violet	Cobalt violet mixed with a bit of alizaran crimson and either raw umber or Prussian blue to deepen and a bit of titanium white. For a lighter shade, add more titanium white.
Red	Alizaran crimson mixed with a bit of titanium white and a bit of raw umber. Combine this shade with the above violet shade for part of each berry.
Green	Deeper leaf color, blended with the violet shade.
Leaves	Permanent green light mixed with a bit each of viridian green, raw umber, and titanium white. Shade leaves with pale yellow or a bit of the violet shade.

Photograph #26

Lesson Pattern

Berries

Begin by painting the violet berry at the upper right of the pattern. The lower half of this berry is undercoated with the lighter violet shade, changing to the deeper violet for the upper half. Lightly dry-brush these shades together. As you undercoat the scalloped outside edges of the berry, slightly pivot the brush so that its outside corner forms semicircles around the entire berry. Clean your brush and put it aside until you are ready to undercoat the next berry.

Pattern #26

Add a drop or two of turpentine to a bit of white so that it is very thin. Using just the tip of your small pointed brush, paint very fine white circles over the entire berry. Begin at an upper side and paint a complete circle of white around each outside scalloped curve. Your brush may pick up some of the berry color, if so, just wipe it lightly in the tissue and add fresh paint to continue. Add each row of thin white circles around the berry in the same manner. Paint these freehand to give a varied effect. Since some of the final center circles may extend over others, lightly dry-brush the center of each circle. A light dry-brushing in these areas will blend in any white irregularities and add extra shading. You may want to dry-brush a small amount of the darker color along the outside darker side so that no white circles show in this area. Don't worry if all the circles are not precisely rounded. They will be prettier if there is some irregularity and blending. When the shading is completed, add very small dots of white to highlight.

Paint and shade all the berries in the suggested shades, or change them to other colors if you like. You could paint them in two shades of green with pale yellow, a deep wine shade with a darker blue, or any other color you like. When you are painting on a light background, you may need to add a slightly darker accent to the light outside area of the berry. To do this, just use the small pointed brush and slightly darker paint to make a fine line of accent color.

Leaves

In this lesson, a little of the berry shade was added to some of the leaf color for an effective contrast. Paint one half of the leaf in the lighter green, and then edge one corner of your brush into the berry shade. Continue to paint the opposite half of the leaf with these two colors blending together. This is a technique you will be using more and more frequently. Carrying the fruit or flower color right into the leaf shading always adds something special to a painting. Be sure the green paint is quite thin as you prepare to add the curliques and vine effect around the berries. Hold the brush almost straight up and down, and use only the tip of it with very thin paint.

Berries and flowers decorate a restored armchair. By Yee Chea Lin.

Dewdrops

Now paint a few dewdrops on the color swatches you prepared earlier. Make the white paint very thin. Use only the tip of the brush to form a circle or a long, narrow drop, if you prefer. Accent the lower part of the dewdrop with a shade deeper than the background color. This, again, should be quite thin and sparingly applied. Add a bit of raw umber to the leaf-green color to deepen the accent color used below the dewdrop. This should generally be applied along the bottom of the dewdrop and slightly around one side, diminishing to nothing. (It is necessary to have this paint also very thin and very lightly applied.) When this is completed, add one or two tiny white dots to suggest a reflected light. When you feel you have mastered the making of dewdrops on your practice swatches, paint them on the berries and leaves, following the lesson design.

After painting all these berries, it should now be easy to paint dewdrops on anything you choose. Paint them in series of two or three, some very small and some large. Remember to deepen the undercoat color so that it shows a slight contrast—giving depth and a suggested shadow to the dewdrop. As long as the background color is dry, you can remove a dewdrop that is not to your liking. Just use a damp brush to lift off the white, and start over. You can also use the point of the damp brush to reduce the amount of darker accent if it seems too pronounced. Use dewdrops for color accents and extra realism. Whenever you can, paint them glistening on fruits, vegetables, and flowers.

LESSON 23

Pansies

This lesson is the last flower you will learn to paint before going on to paint a rose. In this lesson, it is important to fill the brush with two or three colors so that each petal can be completed with just one stroke as it will be in the rose lesson.

These pansies may look a little complicated to paint, but they are really quite easy. The lesson pansies are done in deep shades of purple violet and in pale lavender shades. Some are combined with yellow and some are shaded with just white. You can experiment with the shading and the effects you wish to create. You may prefer to have all your pansies deep in shading, from purple and violet into the deeper blues, or you may prefer pastel shades. Just look at some magazines, flower and seed catalogs, and greeting cards for ideas. You will find pansies represented in such a variety of colors that you'll have no trouble in selecting some.

This pattern is very attractive when painted on tinted parchment paper, using a pale blue wash or another contrasting but soft color for background. A colored background enhances the design and also lets you experiment with various color effects.

Look at Pattern #27 for a moment. All the pansies are spaced apart more than usual so that the construction and shading can be seen more easily. When you paint these flowers a second time, paint the leaves closer to the pansy for more realism. You'll also see that these pansies have both five and six petals. Both types are painted in the same order, beginning with the back petals and moving from left to right (or the reverse if you are left-handed). All the other petals are painted from the inside out, and each petal slightly overlaps the one just painted. The last lower petal is painted with two strokes, one to each side and connecting at the lower front. (Extra half-strokes can be added over the last petal for additional shading.)

Brushes

Pansies and leaves	Large flat brush
Veins, vine effect, and pansy centers	Small pointed brush

Colors

Upper pansy	
Darker shade	Cobalt violet mixed with a bit of Prussian blue.
Lighter shade	Titanium white added to some of the above shade.
Lower petal	Cadmium yellow medium mixed with titanium white and a bit of cobalt violet.
Left pansy	
Darker shade	Cobalt violet mixed with a bit of titanium white to match swatch #31.
Lighter shade	Titanium white added to some of the above shade to match swatch #33.
Right pansy	
Darker shade	Cobalt violet mixed with a bit of alizaran crimson and enough titanium white to match swatch #4.
Lighter shade	Titanium white added to some of the above shade to match swatch #6.
Lower pansy	
All shades except lower petal	Cobalt violet mixed with alizaran crimson and enough titanium white to match swatch #6.
Lower petal	Above yellow shade.
Pansy centers	Ivory black, thinned with turpentine.
Accents	Cadmium yellow medium and titanium white.
Center dot	Cadmium red light.
Leaf shades	
Lighter green	Permanent green light mixed with titanium white and a bit of the violet shades to gray the green.
Darker green	Cobalt violet added to some of the above shade to make a charcoal shade.
Lighten and highlight	Titanium white mixed with cadmium yellow medium to match swatch #21.

Practice

After you have mixed the colors for this lesson, trace the diagram, clip it to your clipboard, and practice the petal shape and its shading. Fill the large flat brush almost full with the deeper shade of violet, stroking into the lighter shade to fill the opposite portion of the brush. As you begin to paint the center back petal, use the same amount of pressure and shaded brush stroke that you used in the rosebud lesson, but guide the inside corner of the brush into a slight dip before continuing the stroke to complete the right half of the petal. Be sure to begin this stroke just inside the outline of petal #2 and end it just inside the outline of petal #3. This is to make sure that you cover the end of each stroke with the next slightly overlapping (#2 and #3) petals. The back petal will look somewhat detached from the pansy unless it is overlapped.

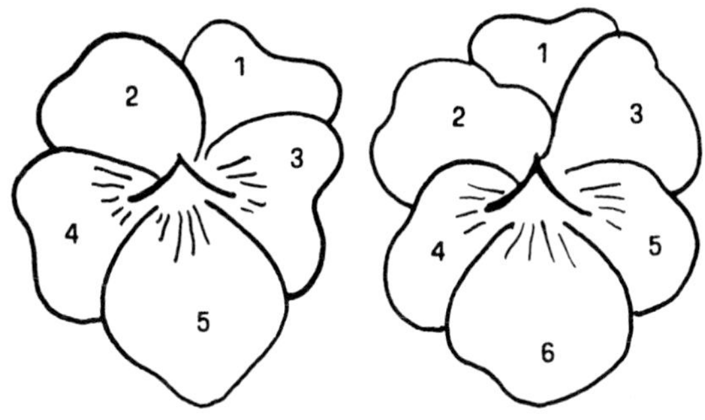

You will probably need to add more paint before painting petals #2 and #3. Without cleaning the brush, just stroke into the same shades to complete each petal. Begin petals #2 and #3 at the inside center, curving the strokes slightly upward (to cover the ends of petal #1) before swinging down to end each stroke beside the next petals to be painted (#4 and #5). The inside corner of the flat brush will be guiding and controlling the angle of these strokes.

Use yellow to shade the lower petal. Do not clean the brush in turpentine, but wipe it in the tissue and allow some of the purple shade to remain in the brush. After filling the brush with the yellow, stroke into the edge of the white once or twice. Leave a slight edge of white on the outside of the brush to separate and shade the lower petal. Begin at the center and curve the stroke downward. Reverse the brush, keeping the white to the outside, and complete the opposite side of the yellow petal. To add more shading, edge with white for two short strokes inside the petal. After painting this pansy, you will see that each new petal must be separated from the one preceding it with either a slightly lighter color or an edge of white, or both.

Photograph #27

Lesson Pattern

Pansies

Now that you have practiced the shading, go ahead and paint the lesson using the same colors (or choose different combinations) and in the same manner. When painting the remaining pansies, do not clean the brush in turpentine but wipe it in tissue before adding the next color over those just used. This produces a gradual soft blending of colors. Only if you would like to have a distinct contrast in colors should you clean the brush in turpentine before adding each new color.

After completing the petals, use the small pointed brush to add the center V of black and the accent dots of yellow and red. The black paint must be very thin and used on only the tip of the brush. Add the thin black paint sparingly to the wide edge of the small flat brush and lightly whisk in the pansy whiskers. Start at the center and then at each side to whisk the black into the petals. It's easier to add more black if needed than it is to remove an excess.

Leaves

And now, for a surprise—no swatch colors are being given for leaf shades. Use your own favorite shades of green. (However, one hint is that a light and a darker green should be used, plus three other colors.) Clean your palette and put some of each of the flower colors into the green shades (a little at a time). Adding a bit of the fruit or flower color to green shades always works beautifully. For a new shading trick, partially fill your brush with a light shade of green and stroke into the edge of one of the pansy colors once or twice. Paint one side of the leaf with this color blending into the green, and contrast the opposite half of the leaf with pale yellow or white. Don't bother to clean your brush in turpentine; just lightly wipe it in the tissue and, again, fill with the green and pansy colors. You may not want to paint all the leaves in this way, but a few will add interest and variety. Just be sure you have a blended light and darker side for each leaf. It is not important to have a sharp contrast between the green shades—rather they should blend softly. The leaves of any composition should not be the most dominant feature but should add a soft attractive background. Of course, if you are painting with bright colors, you will also want your leaves to be a little brighter, but it is never desirable to complete a pastel composition with very bright leaf shades.

After the leaves are painted in, use the small pointed brush to draw in the leaf veins. Remember to thin your paint for this.

Fill-in Flowers

The fill-in flower is added after the leaves have been completed so that a few can be sprinkled over the leaves. This is a perfect place to use the fill-in flower without the stem. It will fill in any open or detached areas and connect the group of pansies. These are painted as before, using a color and white, both on one corner of the flat brush, and lightly dotting the paint in. Sprinkle a few of the fill-in flowers over some of the leaves for a finishing touch.

Photograph #28

OPTIONAL PATTERN

Pansy Design

The pansies, leaves, and blossoms in this design (Pattern #28) are painted with the small flat brush and are perfect for decorating any small object.

Upper Pansies

The two lavender pansies (swatch #6) are shaded with white added to one edge of the brush for contrast and separation of one petal from another. Shade the lower left pansy with both lavender and yellow on the flat brush. To paint the small blossoms, shade both blue and lavender with white. Shade the blue pansy (similar to swatch #8) with white edging each petal. To form the lower petal, add the soft, yellow shade to the blue that is already in the brush and edge it with white.

Leaves

Paint the leaves just as you wish. Then wipe your brush clean and set it aside. Use the small pointed brush and thin darker green paint for stems and veins. Be sure to keep the black paint very thin for the pansy

V and whiskers. To paint the whiskers, slide the edge of the flat brush into the black paint so that only a very little of this color is picked up. Let the pansy dry before you add the black whiskers so that you can remove some of the black if it seems too heavy.

Lower Pansies

Use the small flat brush again for painting the lower pansies and the bud. Shade with the above blue and violet, edging the lower petals with white. Dry-brush blue or violet over the center of the lower petal if you wish a darker accent.

Using blue, violet, and white, paint the bud in a shaded comma stroke. Begin these strokes at the outside and progress into the center. Paint the over-lapping green and white from the stem outward over the bud.

Border

Paint the border with the small pointed brush, using blue, violet, and white. Keep these colors thin enough to flow easily and end with a fine point. Borders often enhance designs and add a finishing touch. They are usually done in a contrasting color or in gold or in a color combined with gold. Painting with gold will be described and used in Lesson 35.

LESSON 24

The Rooster

The rooster is a versatile subject and can be painted in any size, color, or shape. After you have painted the lesson, you will be able to give your imagination full-rein and paint future "kings of the barnyard" in many varied color combinations and for dozens of decorative uses. The rooster in this lesson is painted almost entirely with the large pointed brush, using the small pointed brush only for the eyes and for accenting the beak, legs, and feet. Smaller roosters can easily be painted with the flat brush and will produce almost the same finished effect.

There is a dual purpose in using the pointed brush for this lesson: First, you need a brush that can hold a lot of paint so that a long flowing stroke can be produced without having to refill it; second, you need a brush that will respond to pressure so that you can experience the firm touch needed to fill the outline of the widest part of the tail feathers and the light pressure and gradual lifting of the brush needed to complete the stroke with a fine ending. The amount of pressure applied determines the size of the chest and wing feathers, also. After completing this lesson, you will have gained more skill in using the round pointed brush and will be better able to make the choice between the flat and the round brush for future projects.

Brushes

Rooster	Large pointed brush
Fine detail	Small pointed brush
Rail-grass	Small flat brush

Colors

Fence	Titanium white mixed with a bit of Prussian blue and a bit of raw umber to deepen.
Legs, lower body, and beak	
Lighter shade	Cadmium yellow medium mixed with titanium white and a bit of burnt sienna.
Darker shade	More burnt sienna added to some of the above shade (similar to swatch #44).
Chest, tail feathers, and grass	
Darker shade	Permanent green light mixed with viridian green and enough titanium white to match swatch #34.
Lighter shade	More titanium white added to some of the above green shade.
Wings and tail feathers	
Darker shade	Cadmium red light mixed with titanium white and burnt sienna (similar to swatch #22).
Lighter shade	More titanium white added to some of the above shade (similar to swatch #23).

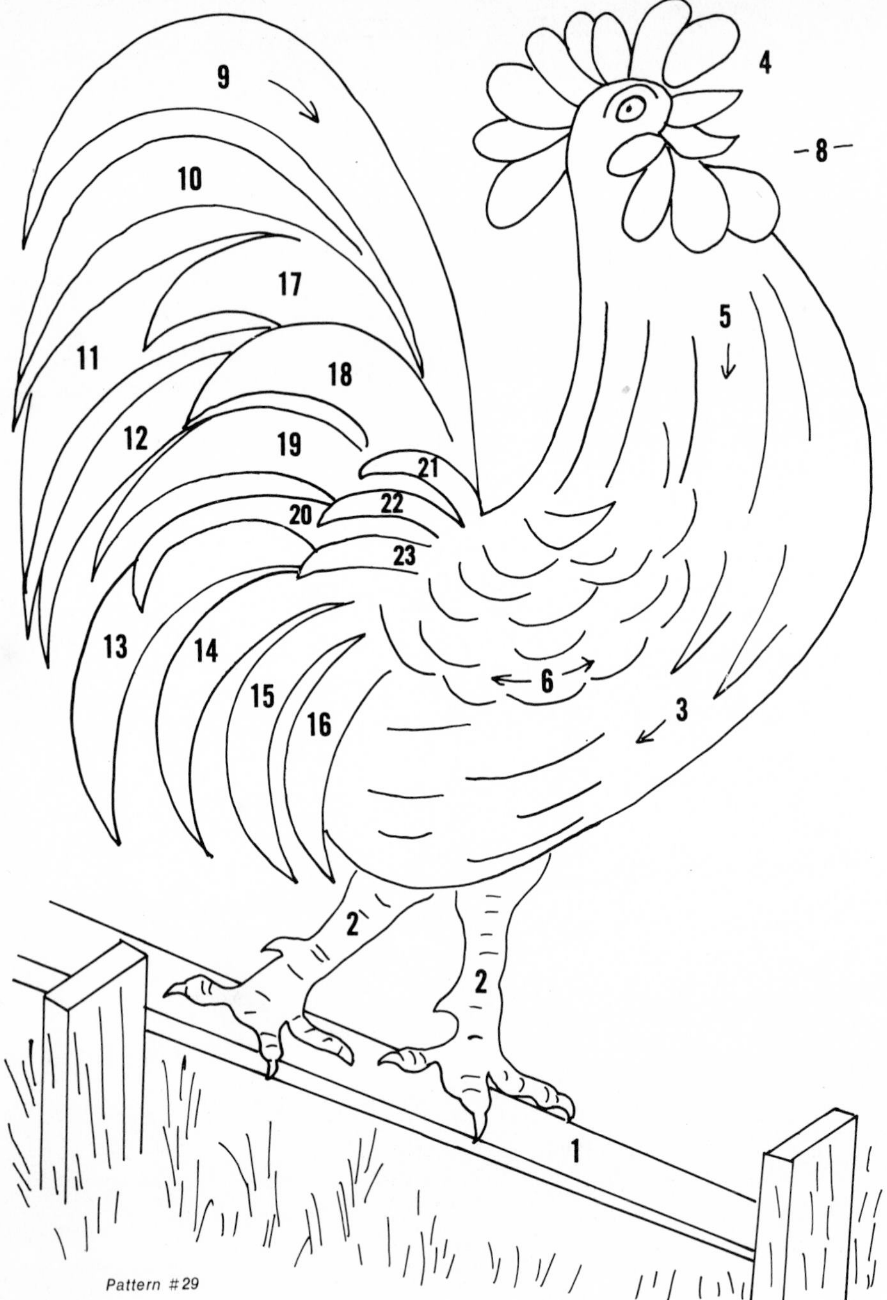

Pattern #29

Comb and wattles	A bit of cadmium red light mixed with Grumbacher red and a bit of titanium white for a bright red shade.
Accent lines of legs, beak, etc.	Burnt umber mixed with titanium white (similar to swatch #51).

Lesson Pattern

Fence

Before painting the rooster, paint the fence he perches on. This is most easily done with the small flat brush. Fill the brush with the suggested shade of blue (or you could also use a red shade, edging one corner of the brush with a little of the brown shade). Paint the top of the long rail, keeping the blue to the inside of the brush and the brown to the outside. Complete the rail and post in the same manner. Notice that the brown automatically shades into the blue, giving the rail a streaked effect. You may want to dry-brush more brown into the blue for a weathered effect. While waiting for the paint to become tacky, you can lightly streak or dry-brush additional thin white paint over the rail. Any color can be dry-brushed over another dry color if it is very thin and lightly applied.

Legs, Lower Body, and Beak

When painting the rooster, you will paint all underneath areas first. Beginning with the legs and feet (area #2 on Pattern #29), paint in order of the numbered sections. To paint the legs and feet, use only the point of the large pointed brush. Fill half the brush with the lighter yellow and half with the deeper yellow. Keeping the darker yellow to the left side, begin to paint the legs from the top to the feet. Wipe the brush in tissue, and lightly dry-brush these colors together to blend. Next, paint the lower body (area #3 on Pattern #29), using the same two shades of yellow and keeping the darker shade to the outside. Be sure your brush is flattened and full of paint as you begin these wide comma strokes. Starting slightly below the upper part of the wing, paint with curved downward strokes ending just under the two feathers marked #15 and #16. Continue these strokes until this area is filled in and shaded around the wing. Add more of the deeper yellow for contrast if you wish. Wipe the brush in tissue, and pick up an edge of deeper yellow to be applied with short comma strokes for the shaded effect. While you still have the yellow shades in your brush, paint in the beak, painting from the wider inside area to the outside.

Chest

Clean your brush and fill it with the two shades of green for area #5. Begin this wide stroke just under the beak, keeping the brighter green to the outside and the lighter green to the inside. Following the curved chest outline, extend the long stroke just over the yellow shades for a feathered ending. You will notice that your brush has picked up a little of the yellow, but this will blend into the green shades quite well. If your brush is completely filled, you will be able to take two or three long shaded strokes before adding more paint. Extend the green strokes slightly into the wing area. Before progressing to the head and left side of the rooster, squeeze the brush in tissue to remove the paint and fill it with the lighter green and yellow. These two shades will produce a slightly lighter color. Dry-brush and blend the head area. To add another layer of feathers, fill the brush with either shade of green, or yellow and green, and edge one side with a small amount of the brown shade. Beginning under the beak and using short strokes, lightly whisk these shades downward over the green. The brown edge of paint will form the additional feather effect. Add as many as you

Photograph #29

wish, and if you don't like the results, you can dry-brush and blend these colors together and start over. You may even prefer this effect and wish to leave it as it is.

Wings

Now paint the wings (area #6), using the deeper coral shade combined with an edge of brown. Paint this by filling the brush with either shade of coral and picking up a very small amount of brown on one side of the brush. These will be painted freehand and will look well any way you paint them. Begin the short curved comma stroke at the lower back of the wing, painting the first scalloped row slightly over the yellow body. End each of the strokes with a fine line extending slightly into the green. Each row of feathers will become a little shorter, with each stroke beginning at the edge of the preceding coral shade. Here, again, you may prefer to undercoat the wing area with the coral shade and then to edge the brush in brown to form the scalloped, curved wings. You also could use white or any other color in place of the brown for the added feathers. You might like to experiment with extending another layer of green feathers slightly over the wing. Roosters can be varied in many ways.

Comb and Wattles

Clean your brush in turpentine before painting the comb and wattles (areas #7 and #8). These are done in two shades: the lighter coral and the bright red, with the red to the outside of the brush and the coral to the inside. Paint from the outside in toward the head, using one stroke to form the smaller part of the comb. Paint the larger comb and wattle with two strokes, keeping the bright red at each side and the lighter coral to the inside. When this is finished, use the small pointed brush without any paint to smooth the light green shade over the base of the comb.

Beak, Legs, and Eye

Lightly outline the beak, legs, and eye, using the small pointed brush containing a little thin brown paint. Paint the eye with white, outlining it in the brown shade and adding a center dot of brown. Add a thin curved line of brown above the eye. Now return to the legs. Use the small pointed brush to outline and dry-brush the darker side of the leg with the brown shade. Add small cross-lines of brown to the legs and feet.

Tail Feathers

Paint the long, fluttering tail feathers in any of the shades on your palette.

In this pattern, a little of the background color shows between some of the feathers. Begin to slowly lift the brush about midway on each feather so that this area remains open. It's very easy to paint each feather right beside the next one, but this often gives a heavy, overladen effect.

Be sure the paint is thinned so that the colors

Rooster design on a Boston rocker. By Yee Chea Lin.

will flow easily together for a blended shading. Begin the wide curved stroke near the wing, and paint outward to a fine ending. Follow the pattern, beginning with #9 through #16 for each of the underneath feathers. The #9 and #10 feathers are painted with the two shades of coral in the brush, edged slightly with the brown. The brush is not cleaned but stroked through the next deeper shade and edged in brown to produce the second deeper shading. Paint feather #11 with the bright red edged in brown. You will need to clean your brush before painting the green shaded feathers (#12 through #16). For these, yellow and the brighter green shade are combined and edged with brown to produce a variety of green shades. Take an extra stroke of brown on the outside of each feather needing contrast or separation from another feather. For the second, lighter layer of feathers (#17 through #20), use the brush filled with the coral and brown shades and stroke into the white for a lighter shade in contrast to the underneath feathers. However, do not paint this layer until all the underneath feathers (#9 through #16) have been completed. As you add the second layer of feathers, be certain that they are in contrast with the feathers underneath them.

To finish any uneven strokes, paint three short comma strokes (#21 through #23) at the base of the wing.

Grass

To paint the grass or a few flowers, use the narrow side of the flat brush or the tip of the large pointed brush. Use shades of green, yellow, and a bit of brown to lightly pounce in the green effect.

When you next paint a rooster, you will know just how to vary the shading and will be able to make your own choice of dominant colors. You can paint this rooster in varying shades of yellow, orange, and brown, or with many shades of blue, pink, and red. Take your choice between very bright, very pastel, or very dark and earthy colors.

LESSON 25

Grapes

Clusters of grapes are usually slower to paint than most fruit groups. They can also show definite brush marks and outlining more than any other fruit. The added brush marks give a rounded effect to the grape, and the outlining is often needed to separate one grape from another. However, when you outline, try to blend the outline color into the grape color whenever possible.

Because everyone has different amounts of patience, some will be content with spending a minimum amount of time in shading grapes. They will choose the "Quick and Easy" Method. Others will be willing to spend a little more time to achieve a more varied shading. They will use the "Happy Medium" Method. And then there are those who enjoy very detailed shading and are happy with nothing less than a perfectly shaded cluster of grapes. They will choose the "Dabbler's Paradise" Method. But, whatever method you finally decide to use, there are several points to remember:

- Many patterns have grapes extending over the leaves. These leaves should be painted first so that they will have a little more drying time before the grapes are painted over them.
- In painting grapes, always complete those first that are underneath or overlapped by other grapes.
- It is best to begin at the lower part of the cluster, completing each underneath grape, before painting the overlapping grapes as you work

upward. Finish shading each grape before beginning the next one. Highlights and deeper accents can be added after the cluster is completed. When you are satisfied with the clusters, give them one or two light sprays of fixative to dry them quickly.

The paint consistency used for grapes is slightly thicker (and less is used in the brush) than for larger fruit. The paint should come from the brush easily enough to form the commas and half-pivots without leaving skipped areas. The paint should cover the background color and also be heavy enough to allow for shading and for dry-brushing.

Since you have painted round cherries in Lessons 16 and 17, the brush movement used to paint round grapes will not be new to you. By now, you have learned how to make the side and corner of the flat brush work for you to paint a great variety of fruit, flowers, and leaves. Painting grapes just becomes a matter of shading another fruit, with a little more time spent to individually shade each grape within a cluster.

Use the trial-sized grape clusters and leaves in Pattern #30 to learn and master all three painting methods. When you finish with the sample patterns, go on to Pattern #31 and paint it in the method you prefer.

"Quick and Easy" Method

This is a quick method for those who enjoy fast painting that has no great detail. It is a satisfactory beginning point for those who have never painted grapes and the basis for learning the more detailed, more realistic "Happy Medium" and "Dabbler's Paradise" methods.

Generally speaking, this method will use two contrasting colors (a light and a darker shade) with white added for shading all blue, purple, and red grapes. Pale yellow is often substituted for the white shading on green, yellow-green, and yellow-brown grapes.

Brushes

All grapes	Small flat brush

Colors

Blue grapes	
Lighter shade	Titanium white mixed with Prussian blue to match swatch #8.
Darker shade	Prussian blue mixed with titanium white to match swatch #7.
Highlight	Titanium white.
Blue-purple grapes	
Lighter shade	Prussian blue mixed with titanium white to match swatch #8.
Darker shade	Cobalt violet, just as it comes from the tube or thinned with only one drop of turpentine.
Highlight	Titanium white.

Lesson Pattern

Trace Pattern #30, Part 2. All the grapes marked X are partially underneath other grapes and should be shaded before the overlying grapes.

- Pick up just enough light blue #8 to paint a comma the width of the small brush along the dotted line on the left side of grape 1X.
- Wipe the brush with the rag and pick up just enough deeper blue #7 to paint another comma on the right side of grape 1X.
- Wipe the brush and pick up a bit of white, placing a dab in the center area between the two shades of blue.

- Wipe the brush and lightly blend the colors together, keeping the light and dark areas connected by a gradual blending. Wipe the brush frequently while dry-brushing.
- Don't overwork the grape shading. Use as few brush movements as possible when dry-brushing. Let the brush marks show. They help give contrast and contour to the grape.
- Lighten the center with a bit of white brushed lightly across the grape to give a rounded effect. The highlights can be added when the cluster is completed. On small grapes, just a dot of white, or a small streak, is usually sufficient to suggest light reflecting off the grapes.

Continue painting each of the grapes in this manner. Keep the lighter color to the left and the deeper color to the right so that each grape will be shaded from light to dark and so that the overall shading of the cluster will show the contrast of light against dark.

Wipe your brush, set aside the pattern you painted, and trace the same pattern, Part 2, for the next sample. Paint the blue-purple grapes, using the same method, and contrast the light blue with cobalt violet. A third, very deep shade of violet can be used as an accent color to separate one grape from another. To mix the third deeper shade, use the cobalt violet and deepen it with a bit of Prussian blue, alizaran crimson, or both. These shades of blue and violet are used for you to see how much contrast is necessary to have between any two shades you may later choose to use. You have learned in previous lessons how to vary the shades of blue or violet by adding red, blue, or brown to deepen or more white to lighten. Change these colors in any way you choose, but keep a definite contrast.

"Happy Medium" Method

Now you will use the same pattern (Part 2) to paint with different colors and a different method.

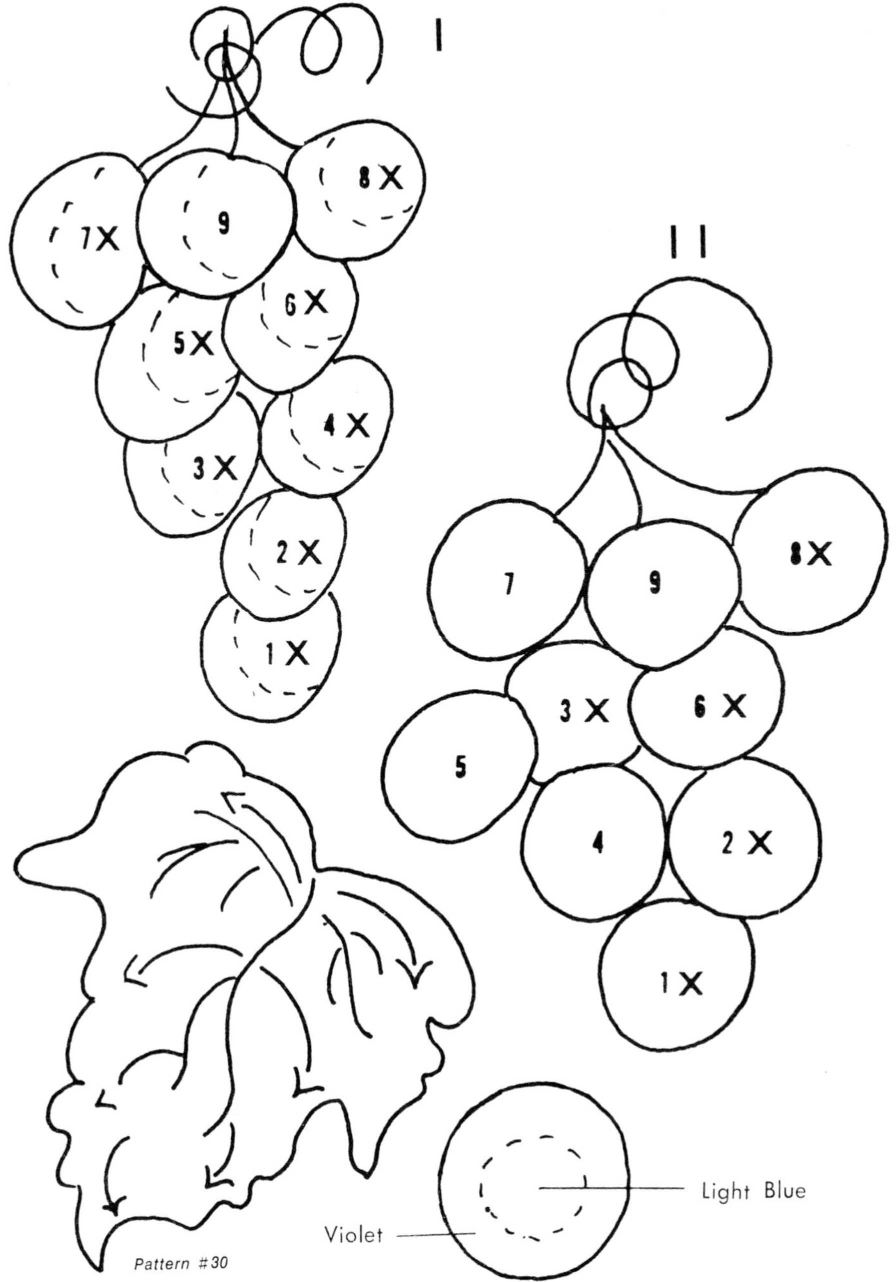

Pattern #30

Brushes

Grapes	Small flat brush
Accent lines	Small pointed brush

Colors

Grapes

Lighter shade	Cadmium yellow medium, thinned with turpentine.
Darker shade	A bit of burnt umber or burnt sienna added to some of above shade to match swatches #44 or #45.
Outsides	Permanent green light mixed with viridian green and titanium white to match swatch #34. Vary the green by adding raw umber, burnt umber, or burnt sienna to deepen. Permanent green light or viridian green can be used alone and deepened with the brown colors.
Centers	Titanium white.
Deeper accents	Permanent green light mixed with a bit of burnt umber. Dry-brush a bit of burnt sienna over some of the grapes if desired.
Lighter accents	Cadmium yellow medium mixed with enough titanium white to match swatch #21.
Highlights	Titanium white.

Photograph #31

Lesson Pattern

The pattern shows grape 3X overlapped by four other grapes so that only a portion of it is seen. The hidden grape 3X should be darker than the others. As you paint this grape, use darker paint to make about three press-strokes along the upper overlapped area. Paint a slightly lighter color in the lower left area and lightly blend the two colors together. Grapes 4, 5, 6X, and 9 will each have the lighter side extending over the darker hidden grape for the necessary contrast. In the future when you find several hidden or partial grapes in a cluster, you will know how to shade them.

The "Happy Medium" Method begins by painting a small yellow grape in the center of each separate grape outline. It is then encircled by two comma strokes of the green shade.

- Paint the inside small grape with the yellow, using two connecting, half-pivot strokes.
- Wipe the brush and pick up the green paint, placing the brush just outside the yellow grape outline. Paint a curved comma stroke on each side of the grape.
- Wipe the brush and blend the two colors together as in the "Quick and Easy" Method.
- Dry-brush more yellow in the center area of the grape if you want a more pronounced yellow shading.
- The third deeper shade should be added now to produce both a deeper accent to some of the grapes and a more varied shading effect.
- Burnt sienna may be added very sparingly to just one corner of the brush and used to lightly outline any grape needing more contrast along the lower (or dark) area. (Add just a drop or two of turpentine to thin the burnt sienna.) You may find it necessary to separate the light and dark areas of one grape from another. Either use the corner of the flat brush with very little brown, or try using the small pointed brush to add the accent line. Be sure to blend and dry-brush the accent line up into the grape color.
- Use the pale yellow shade to paint very short, curved commas across the grape where a light coloring is desired.
- When the cluster is completed, add the white highlights.

You have shaded this cluster from dark to light so that each grape will have a blended contrast of these opposite shadings. Only a bit of burnt sienna dry-brushed over the damp grape colors will produce added coloring to the grape. It also will enable you to see how the use of a third, deep color will improve any cluster of grapes, giving it added depth and coloring. In the "Quick and Easy" Method, you painted with only three colors—a light, a dark, and white. In the "Happy Medium" Method, you've used a light, a dark, and a very dark color while adding brown, pale yellow, and white for additional coloring.

"Dabbler's Paradise" Method

Do not try painting grapes by this method until you have tried the first two methods. For this method, trace and have ready Part 1 of Pattern #30.

Before you begin painting, decide upon which will be the light and which will be the dark side of the cluster. For instance, you may choose to imagine light coming from the upper left of your design. The grapes lying near the imaginary light would be shaded in very light colors. Those below them would be slightly darker, and the grapes that are partially hidden, or lower in the design, would be even darker.

The colors suggested for this practice lesson will produce a green grape, shaded to a very pale yellow. Dry-brushing burnt sienna over the deeper green mixture will accent the darker grapes or add color to the lighter green grapes. Even though a grape may be predominantly dark, it will often need a lighter color accent or highlight on one side to help separate it from the other grapes. The "Happy Medium" Method could be used to apply these colors. You might also try undercoating the entire grape, beginning with the lowest grape in the cluster and adding the darker and lighter shades just as you did when painting larger fruit. When you have finished, go on to paint the grape leaf. You will then be ready to paint any cluster of grapes in any color combination.

Brushes

Grapes and leaves	Small flat brush
Accent lines and veins	Small pointed brush

Colors

Grapes	
Lighter shade	Permanent green light mixed with a bit of cadmium yellow medium and titanium white.
Darker shade	Viridian green mixed with a bit of raw umber.
Lighter accent	Cadmium yellow medium mixed with titanium white to match swatch #21.
Deeper accent	Burnt sienna.
Highlight	Titanium white.
Leaves	Permanent green light mixed with a bit of raw umber and titanium white (similar to swatch #38).
Darker shading color	Raw umber, softened with turpentine.
Lighter shading color	Cadmium yellow medium mixed with enough titanium white to match swatch #21.
Veins	Above shade of dark green, accented with raw umber and pale yellow.

Lesson Pattern

Leaves

Grape leaves are painted more quickly and easily than the grapes. Referring to practice Pattern #30, use the small flat brush to paint the leaves and the small pointed brush to lightly paint the veins, using a deeper shade of green.

This leaf, which is painted in a different manner from any that you have painted before, will become a very attractive leaf in a short time. Lift aside a little of the green shade, and add a drop or two of turpentine to thin it slightly. Use the large flat brush to paint large leaves and the small flat brush to paint smaller leaves. Dip the flat brush in the thinner green paint and begin at the center top to follow the leaf outline along the entire left side. Repeat this on the right side.

Holding the brush flat against the leaf outline, paint just inside the leaf with a very slight left-to-right movement. This, which is called "squiggling," gives a thin irregular outline just the width of the brush. Although it is thin and irregular, it holds the leaf outline and also serves as a partial undercoat. Your brush will not leave the pattern to paint any stroke, but will tip on the outside corner to form the curved, irregular edges of the leaf. Wipe the brush and fill it with the green paint. Beginning at the inside center of the leaf, use short strokes that curve up, then slightly down, to follow the leaf contour. Stop just short of the squiggled outline as you continue filling in the entire leaf. Don't worry about how many strokes you take to fill in the leaf. More short strokes give a better shaded and textured effect.

Use the yellow paint in the flat brush to lighten one half of the leaf. These, too, will be short strokes, with the outside corner of the brush doing the work. To lighten the outside edge of the leaf, begin slightly beyond the center vein line and add the pale yellow over the green in short strokes. Let the pale yellow show slightly beyond the green along the outside upper

curves of the leaf. The additional ye[illegible]
added in one of two ways:

- With a small amount of yellow p[illegible] place the brush just inside t[illegible] squiggled line. Paint as many s[illegible] the outside in, as you need[illegible] shaded effect. Paint these o[illegible] shades so that the strokes wi[illegible] fine line of yellow will show t[illegible] You may also want to add m[illegible] pale yellow on the leaf for a[illegible]
- Reverse the above method [illegible] strokes, to paint from insid[illegible] the outside curves of the le[illegible] give the leaf a slightly irre[illegible]

The darker accent can [illegible] side of the leaf in the same manner, usin[illegible] thinned with a few drops of turpentine. Be sure you have some of the leaf-green color in your brush before adding a little of the brown to a portion of the brush. Keep the brown on the upper side of the brush as you add the dark shading. Take additional short-curved strokes near the center vein if you feel the leaf needs more dark shading. In place of the additional short strokes of brown, you could also lightly dry-brush the deeper color over the center area. Dry-brushing other colors over the wet green leaf shade always adds a pleasant and varied shading.

Use the small pointed brush with thin dark green paint to lightly paint in a few leaf veins. These should be very thin, delicate lines curving slightly downward and ending just beyond the center of the leaf. Lightly accent a few veins with the brown or yellow.

Now you are ready to paint the grape cluster shown in Photograph #31, using the method of your choice and Pattern #31. Use your own choice of blue-purple colors for the grapes (the color suggestions under the "Quick and Easy" Method will give you a

Pattern #31

starting point) and the greens that you have just used for painting the leaves.

Almost any shade of green will blend with the blue-purple grapes in Photograph #31. Here, permanent green light is added to white to match swatch #37. Both sides of the leaf are painted in the same shade of green. The dark side of the leaf is accented with raw umber, and the light side with pale yellow (and some white if needed).

Ornamental tray incorporating lesson on grapes, apples, pears, daisy-type flowers, and basic comma strokes. By Yee Chea Lin.

Photograph #32

LESSON 26

Cherubs

For centuries, both classical and folk artists have painted cherubs as being imaginary, curvacious, and winged figures floating amidst clouds, flowers, and trailing ribbons. Decorative cherubs are frequently painted on furniture, walls, or metal and wood items. They also are often used to decorate items for special occasions (especially Valentine's Day), and announcements of weddings and births.

Brushes

Entire cherub, wings, hair, clouds, flowers, and leaves	Small flat brush
Body outline and all fine detail	Small pointed brush
Ribbon and bow	Large pointed brush

Colors

Cherub	
Body	Bit of Grumbacher red or alizaran crimson mixed with a bit of burnt sienna and titanium white (similar to swatch #24).
Shading	A bit more red and burnt sienna added to some of the above shade (slightly deeper than swatch #60).
Outline	Titanium white mixed with burnt sienna to match swatch #59.
Hair	
Lighter shade	Cadmium yellow medium mixed with a bit of titanium white.
Deeper shade	A bit of burnt umber, a bit of burnt sienna, and titanium white added to some of the above shade (similar to swatch #52).
Highlight	Titanium white.
Ribbon and bow, clouds, wings	Viridian green mixed with enough titanium white to match swatch #11, shaded and contrasted with titanium white.
Flowers and leaves	Small amounts of cobalt violet, alizaran crimson, cadmium yellow medium, and permanent green light mixed with titanium white.

Lesson Pattern

Body

The consistency of the two flesh-toned paint colors should be a bit thick as it will be more heavily applied than usual in order to thoroughly cover any contrasting background color. Use the small flat brush to undercoat the entire cherub with the lighter flesh tone. After this is completed, lightly wipe the brush in the lap rag before adding the deeper flesh tone to about half of the brush width. Keeping the deeper shade to the outside of the brush, begin to outline and catch in the undercoat with this shade. Begin at the forehead, curving around the face and into the neck. Blend and drybrush each area before continuing to add the contrasting color around the cupid's body. As you paint, you may wish to add more of the deeper shade to suggest darker shadows along the curved areas on one side of the figure.

Pattern #32

When this is completed, use your small pointed brush to make a smooth outline and to blend in the brown shade #59 around the figure. In the future, you may want to outline and accent the figure with gold paint, even adding a bit of gold to the hair. You will always need to accent the outline of the cherub—especially when painting on a very light background color. Whenever you have a darker background color, you will need to paint the figure with thicker and more heavily applied paint.

Hair

While the cherub's figure is drying, mix the colors used for the hair and complete this detail. Fill the small flat brush with both the yellow and brown hair shades. The curls are formed by a light half or quarter pivot of the brush. Use the upper or right corner of the brush to form the ringlets at the outside of the head. Use the lower or left corner to form the hairline around the face. You can better control the shape of the head if you paint well inside the outer hairline while adding extra pivots to balance the general shape. Just a few extra strokes beyond the pattern can quickly make the head too large. When the curls are completed, wipe the brush lightly and pick up the white on one corner of the brush. Add a few light pivots of white for highlights and additional shading.

Ribbon and Bow

Next, mix the paints used for the ribbon and bow. Paint these bows with two strokes (as in Lesson 11), using the large pointed brush filled with aqua and white paint. The first section of the ribbon begins under the flowers and curves slightly downward before turning to join the longer, flowing ribbon.

The second, wider section of the ribbon is painted with two wide strokes. The first stroke should swing upward to complete the half of the ribbon extending over the body and should then curve beyond to a fine point. To add the second stroke smoothly, begin at the same point of the first stroke, overlapping slightly, and swing the stroke downward before curving up over the body and out to a fine ending. Keep the edge of white to the upper side of your brush as the second stroke is added so that it will show a turned effect against the above aqua ribbon. The ribbon will be more effective if the aqua shade is against the body and the white and lightly shaded aqua is kept to the center areas. Resume the shaded stroke below the cherub's knee and paint outward to a turned ribbon ending.

Clouds

The clouds are painted with a shaded pivot of the small flat brush. Use white and pale aqua in the brush to form the clouds using the same motion you did to paint the cupid's ringlets. Pile them in overlapping layers, and lightly whisk the colors together for an effect that is pleasing to you.

Wings

The wings are painted with the narrow side of the small flat brush, with both aqua and white used for a shaded stroke. Using short strokes, paint these from the outside of the wing into the body. Use the side of the flat brush to paint the upper wing curve, again stroking from the body outward to the wing tip. Because these wings are too small for much detail, they need only suggest wings. The detailed shading and construction of larger wings will be described later in the lesson on federal designs.

Flowers

To complete the design, paint the flowers and leaves with your small flat brush and extend them over the bows. Use your small pointed brush to add the fine green sprigs falling beside the ribbon.

You can vary this design to fit your decorative needs by reversing the pattern so that the cherub is facing right. Try using two of them in a design if you wish. Change the ribbon and cloud colors as you like to compliment the background color you are using.

Photograph #33

LESSON 27

Lemons and Limes

Except for the colors, lemons and limes are painted in the same way as any fruit that you have painted. The textured appearance is made by utilizing a new technique—using either a very small piece of sponge or an old piece of terry cloth. You may also use the brush to produce a heavily stippled effect on the lemons and a lighter texture on the limes. Add only a drop or two of turpentine to the undercoat colors as you will need a rather heavy base in order to achieve the necessary textured appearance of the finished fruit.

Brushes

Lemons, limes, and leaves	Large flat brush
Branches and blossoms	Small flat brush
Leaf and branch accents	Small flat brush

Colors

Lemons

Undercoat	Cadmium yellow medium mixed with a bit of titanium white (and a bit of green to match swatch #34 if desired).
Right sides	Cadmium yellow medium mixed with a bit of burnt sienna and a bit of titanium white (similar to swatch #48).
Left sides	Permanent green light mixed with viridian green and enough titanium white to match swatch #34.
Lighten	Titanium white (applied with sponge or terry cloth or stippled with brush).

Limes

Undercoat	Permanent green light mixed with viridian green and enough titanium white to match swatch #34.
Darker accent	A bit of Prussian blue added to a bit of the above shade.
Lighten	Cadmium yellow medium mixed with enough titanium white to match swatch #21 (applied with sponge or terry cloth or stippled). Titanium white highlight added if desired.

Branch	Burnt umber mixed with burnt sienna and enough titanium white to match swatch #51.
Darker accents	Burnt umber.
Lighter accents	Titanium white.

Leaves

Lighter shade	Above shade #34.
Darker shade	Burnt sienna added to some of the above shade.
Yellow-green	Above yellow shade #21 with green shades.

Stems and veins	Above deeper green leaf shade.
Blossoms	Titanium white, thinned with turpentine, dry-brushed with a bit of pale green.
Centers	Yellow.
Accents	Brown.

Lesson Pattern

Lemons

Begin by looking closely at Pattern #33. Notice that in the cluster of three lemons, you'll paint the smaller, underneath lemon first. Start painting by undercoating this partial lemon. Wipe the brush in the lap rag, pick up a small amount of the yellow-brown shade on one corner of the flat brush, and lightly accent the right side of the lemon. Again, wipe the color from your brush, and on one corner, add a small amount of the green shade. Dry-brush the shadow area into the wet yellow undercoat and around the leaf. As in all clusters of fruit, the fruit that is underneath the others should be a little darker so that it will look more realistic. When the shading is complete, dip the sponge or piece of terry cloth, lightly into some white and apply it in small dabs and pounces for a slightly textured appearance. When this is complete, accent the outer edges of the lemon very slightly with the yellow-brown shade. You may prefer to use the small flat brush on the partial lemon since it is a small area to work on.

Paint the two overlying lemons next. Since they will not dry too quickly, you may undercoat them both at once. Be sure to apply the undercoat liberally because dry-brushing, sponging, and blending for a textured appearance will remove some of the paint.

Pattern #33

When the undercoating is completed, shade the lemon to the left of the pattern. Pick up the yellow-brown shade on one corner of the flat brush, and using a very light touch, accent the entire right side. Wipe the brush, pick up a corner of the green shade, and accent the left side of the lemon with this color, dry-brushing lightly and blending into the lemon. Then use the sponge or small piece of cloth to apply the white very lightly for a textured appearance. Proceed in the same manner for the lemon to the left of your pattern.

You may prefer to use your brush to dabble on a bit of the white and then use the sponge or the piece of terry cloth to give the desired effect. Or, you may pick up the paint right on the cloth or sponge and apply it to the surface very lightly. It may be necessary to re-accent the edges of the lemon with a little paint on the corner of the brush to make the outline of the fruit sharp and clear. The drier (or more tacky) the paint becomes, the easier it becomes for you to achieve texture. It's a lot of fun to dabble and shade in any way you choose. You may prefer a very high, piled, textured effect with the white or a smoother effect that blends the colors together. The choice is yours. When the entire shading is completed, use your small pointed brush, with a tiny amount of green paint, to add a fine line of accent to the knobby base and upper outline of each lemon. A bit of white may also be used in order to highlight.

Limes

The limes will be undercoated with the blue-green shade you have mixed, and will be sponged for a lighter effect with the very pale yellow shade. In addition, you will need to add a small amount of Prussian blue to a bit of the blue-green shade for a deeper shadow along the inside areas of each lime. You may even prefer to soften a bit of the Prussian blue with turpentine and use it very sparingly over the wet, green undercoating for a more distinct shadow. Sponge very lightly for the textured effect, as too much pressure will remove the undercoat color. If this happens, re-apply the blue-green shade and start over. After each of the two limes are completed, add some extra darkening along the darker sides. Straighten out any edges that may be irregular by adding a bit of the blue-green or lighter green to the corner of your brush and sliding it gently along the outer edges to give a smooth line.

Branches and Leaves

The branch will be painted using the shades of brown you prefer or the suggested shades given above. Deepen with a darker brown, and lighten and highlight with white.

Use a variety of green in your leaf shading, beginning with the blue-green used for the limes. When painting the leaves, fill the brush with the shade of green you want, adding the deeper shade to one edge for the darker side of the leaf. Pick up the pale yellow or white added to the green already on your brush for the opposite, lighter half of the leaf. All the leaf veins are lightly applied with a darker green paint rather than a brown shade.

Blossoms

Use the small flat brush to paint the white blossoms. Dry-brush a bit of pale green into the white blossoms, and finish by adding the brown accent lines around the yellow centers with the small pointed brush. Use thicker, white paint to produce a little heavier blossom on darker backgrounds.

LESSON 28

Bugs, Butterflies, and Mushrooms

This collage of bright and colorful bugs, butterflies, and mushrooms is painted in whimsical colors and can be separated and/or combined in any way you wish. You will most often use them as a part of another design to add other colors, help fill out a pattern, or perhaps add a note of surprise or amusement. The butterflies, which can easily be used to decorate a great variety of household objects, look especially nice on children's room walls, furniture, and kitchen cabinets. Some of the brightly colored mushrooms and bugs can be used on wood panels, waste baskets, or small buckets and pails. They make gay and amusing designs for children's gifts, too. Look through your patterns and your home to see how you can include these to fit special areas.

Butterflies:

(A) Wings and body	Cobalt violet mixed with enough titanium white to match swatch #31.
Accents	Ivory black and titanium white.
Gold shade	Cadmium yellow medium mixed with burnt sienna and enough titanium white to match swatch #44 or gold paint.
(B) Upper wings and body	Cadmium yellow medium mixed with enough titanium white to match swatch #55.
Lower wings	Cadmium yellow medium mixed with enough titanium white to match swatch #19.
Lower wing detail	Black ink.
Lower wing accents	Cadmium yellow medium mixed with a bit of burnt sienna and enough titanium white to match swatch #44 or gold paint.
(C) Inside wings	Prussian blue mixed with enough titanium white to match swatch #8.
Comma and dots	Cadmium yellow medium mixed with enough titanium white to match swatch #19.
Outside wing color and body	Cobalt violet mixed with enough titanium white to match swatch #32.
(D) Outside wings	Permanent green light mixed with titanium white.

Inside wings	Prussian blue mixed with enough titanium white to match swatch #8.
Body	Alizaran crimson mixed with enough titanium white to match swatch #28.
Accent lines	Ivory black, thinned with turpentine, or black ink.

Bugs:

(1) Large mushroom Stem and top	Burnt sienna mixed with alizaran crimson and enough titanium white to match swatch #26.
Shading	Above shade with enough titanium white added to match swatch #25.
Underside	Cadmium yellow medium mixed with burnt sienna and enough titanium white to match swatch #44.
Green worm body	Permanent green light mixed with a bit of Grumbacher red and enough titanium white to match swatch #38.
Green worm spots	Cadmium yellow medium mixed with permanent green light and enough titanium white to match swatch #41.
Green worm accents	Yellow and black.
Green worm hat	Ivory black.
Green worm hat accent	Titanium white.
(2) Small mushroom Stem	Burnt sienna mixed with alizaran crimson and enough titanium white to match swatch #26.
Shading	Above shade mixed with titanium white to match swatch #25.
Top	Green shade #39.
Circles	Permanent green light mixed with a bit of Grumbacher red and enough titanium white to match swatch #38.
Underside	Cobalt violet mixed with alizaran crimson to match swatch #5.
Ladybug body	Cadmium yellow mixed with cadmium red light and enough

	titanium white to match swatch #55.
Ladybug shaded sides	Cadmium yellow medium mixed with cadmium red light, a bit of viridian green, and enough titanium white to match swatch #49.
Ladybug spots and legs	Ivory black.
(3) Small mushroom Stem	Cadmium yellow medium mixed with a bit of burnt umber and enough titanium white to match swatch #46; above color with enough titanium white added to match swatch #45.
Underside	Cobalt violet with enough titanium white added to match swatch #32.
Top	Prussian blue with enough titanium white added to match swatch #8.
Circles	Titanium white.
(4) Small mushroom Stem	Cobalt violet mixed with alizaran crimson and enough titanium white to match swatch #5.
Shading	Above shade with enough titanium white added to match swatch #4.
Underside	Cadmium yellow medium mixed with cadmium red light to match swatch #55.
Top	Cadmium yellow medium mixed with enough titanium white to match swatch #19.
(5) Small mushroom Stem	Burnt sienna mixed with alizaran crimson and enough titanium white to match swatch #26.
Shading	Above color with enough titanium white added to match swatch #25.
Underside	Cobalt violet with enough titanium white added to match swatch #32.
Top	Cobalt violet mixed with alizaran crimson and enough titanium white to match swatch #5.
Spots	Grumbacher red with enough titanium white added to match swatch #3.

Photograph #34

Lesson Pattern

The small flat brush is most easily used to paint most of the mushrooms, bugs, and butterflies. Use the large flat or pointed brush whenever the design is large enough for either of these brushes. Use the small pointed brush for small dots, circles, and lines. You will find that the longer you paint, the more you will find a need for in-between-size brushes and will know at a glance which size brushes will do the best work for the design you are painting. Since some of the strokes on the butterfly wings are easier to paint with a pointed brush that is in-between the small and large brush in size, now is the time to buy one. You may also want to get a flat brush that is half as large as your small flat brush. And, of course, should you want to paint very large designs on walls or furniture, you'll need larger brushes than you now have.

Some of the butterfly detail is accented with black. Use your pen and ink to outline these details, wait a few minutes, and then paint the color over the ink. The black lines will show through the paint enough to re-accent when the paint is dry.

a
d
b
c
1
2
3
4
5
Pattern #34

LESSON 29

Antiquing

Simply stated, antiquing is the process of applying a thin coat of dark paint and then wiping it off. Achieving a professional effect, however, requires more than this—it requires much time to be spent in blending, wiping, or dry-brushing the antiqued finish to create a pleasing effect of light and dark areas.

Originally, antiquing was done by blending shades of thin brown paint onto painted or stained surfaces of wood or metal to create an illusion of age. Brown shades were used because they more nearly approached the tone of the normal aging process, marked by the accumulation of grime and by worn finishes. In our twentieth-century homes, however, painted furniture has become very popular, and paint manufacturers have developed hundreds of durable colors to compliment every possible interior color scheme. Because of the variety of background colors available, you are able to antique with other combinations of colors for a variety of interesting effects. However, one rule remains the same in all antiquing: Always antique with a color that is darker than the background color. A light color brought over a dark color is not antiquing at all, but only a novelty effect.

Antiquing may be done either before or after the object has been decorated. When antiquing before the design is painted, apply the mixture lightly. After the design has been completed, you can add more antiquing color.

Although the antiquing mixture contains some varnish, it is not enough to make the antique coat permanent. It needs to be finished with a coat of varnish, shellac, or spray fixative for durability. Varnish and shellac will give a slightly yellow color to the finish, but this will not be noticeable on any color but white. These are more generally used on furniture, walls, or objects subject to daily wear. Wood and metal objects used for decorative and ornamental purposes can be more quickly finished by using a spray fixative, which is clear and doesn't yellow. This is the same spray fixative called for in previous lessons to hasten drying time of any painted design. It is just as successfully used to seal antiquing or stained wood colors quickly.

There are as many antiqued effects as there are people who create them. Some very lightly antique the finished object, showing the background color almost in its original shade. Others prefer having a heavy deposit of the antiquing color, which produces a weathered, aged effect. A light coating of the antiquing color will scarcely change the overall background color, showing more heavily on only the outer areas, whereas a heavy application, with little removed, will completely change the background color.

Semigloss paint is the ideal surface for antiquing; flat, or dull, paint is also easily antiqued. The slick surface of a high-gloss enamel or lacquer is difficult to antique and should be avoided. Stained wood, sealed with a low-luster varnish or spray fixative, can also be antiqued.

Make any antiquing color you want—easily and inexpensively—by mixing tube oil colors with turpentine and a little linseed oil or varnish. The addition of varnish or oil adds body to the mixture and also causes it to dry more slowly. This allows more time to wipe, blend, or dry-brush for the finished effect. The above ingredients are all you will ever need to produce an antiquing mixture in your color choice. First, experiment with small amounts of antiquing colors, using them on small objects. Try several different colors or one color over another. If you don't like the effect, wipe it off immediately with turpentine and begin anew. Apply the mixture with a brush or a small rag. If you use a rag, you may want to wear rubber gloves to protect your hands. As soon as the antiquing mixture is applied, wipe lightly and blend with either smooth or coarse textures.

Smooth Textures

To blend smoothly and to remove excess mixture, use a soft cloth and wipe with the grain (or lengthwise). Use an inexpensive, synthetic bristle brush for dry-brushing and blending, wiping it frequently on a large rag. When dry-brushing, work from the center areas out to the corners. Leave the outside and corners darker, gradually shading to almost no color in the center areas. If you should remove too much color, just reapply the mixture and let it stand awhile longer before dry-brushing.

The center area of any antiqued object or piece of furniture should always be the lightest. Through wear, these areas on chairs, tables, and chests become lighter in color, with darker areas remaining along the side edges, in the corners, and in any grooves and carved areas. Even after the antiquing is finished, add a little more of the mixture to further accent these areas.

There are two tricks to using the dry-brush technique for antiquing, and neither is difficult:

- Don't bear down on the brush. Using a light pressure, quickly flip the wrist in a back-and-forth motion.
- Wipe the brush frequently in a large cloth. Unless the brush is wiped often to remove excess color, you will only be spreading the color around instead of blending it.

Coarse Textures

Coarse textures produce a streaked, dark effect. To achieve this effect, lightly wipe with a square of turkish towel; an old ribbed, cotton undershirt or sock; or a coarse, bristle paintbrush. You will probably want to try your hand at several of these methods for variety.

The following list of antiquing mixes are only a few of the many you can mix and use alone or over other shades. These are given in small amounts—the quantities may be increased for antiquing larger objects. The consistency of the antiquing mixture should be similar to that of thick cream, achieved by using approximately one teaspoon of varnish and three teaspoons of turpentine mixed with each of the following oil colors:

- *Brown:* 1 inch burnt umber. Vary by adding more burnt umber.
- *Brown:* ½ inch burnt umber and ½ inch raw umber. Permanent green light or more of the brown shades may be added for variety.
- *Brown:* 1 inch burnt sienna. Raw umber may be added for a deeper shade. Vary by adding more burnt sienna.
- *Yellow-green:* ½ inch permanent green light mixed with 1 inch cadmium yellow medium and ½ inch raw umber to deepen. This mixture can be lightly rubbed over any object previously antiqued in the brown shades.
- *Blue-green:* ½ inch permanent green light mixed with ½ inch viridian green and ivory black to deepen.
- *Dusky mauve:* ½ inch alizaran crimson mixed with a bit of Prussian blue and a bit of raw umber. The shade of mauve can be varied by using more or less blue or brown.
- *Black:* Ivory black thinned with the antiquing mixture.
- *Blue-black:* Grumbacher red mixed with Prussian blue and raw umber. Vary this by adding more Prussian blue.

A very old subdued coloring effect can be achieved by bringing the antiquing color completely over the painted design and wiping it off immediately. Reapply if a deeper shading is desired.

Throughout the lessons, you have added some

of the flower or fruit color to the leaves for harmonious blending or the tying together of the painted design. Now, by using antiquing, you will take another step toward the tying together of the design and background. To do this, soften small amounts of the straight oil colors used in the design with a few drops of turpentine or with the varnish and turpentine mixture. (This will be slightly thicker than the mixture used for antiquing.) Apply the colors with a small brush or a square of cloth —one color over another—and blend with another smooth or textured cloth or brush. You can do this directly over previously antiqued, dry surfaces to surfaces that have not been antiqued or to lightly stained wood.

On small objects, some prefer to finish blending the colors with their fingertips. This can be messy, but it produces the desired effect. Quickly dry each additional shading with spray fixative, which also serves as a finish coat for the decorated object.

Suggested Background Colors

The color you select to paint your metal or wood item will be influenced by the color of the room in which it is to be used. Visit your paint store and look through the colors of ready-mixed, semigloss paint in half-pint cans through gallon sizes. Ivory, white, and off-white are always safe colors to select since they can be antiqued easily in any color. These colors can also be used to mix the small amounts of paint needed for several small items. Just pour a little of the paint into a small container and add to it your tube oil color (or colors). Mix and stir well to dissolve any lumps before adding more white or off-white. Thin slightly if necessary. The colors you have learned to mix throughout your lessons will be of great value when you begin mixing various shades of background paint.

There are also many good background colors available in spray paints. Read the directions carefully on each can before using.

Antiqued folk-art dish.
Courtesy Joyce W. Hundley, Dutch Village.

In addition to ivory or white, any pastel shade —pink, blue, yellow, green, beige, or violet—can be lightly antiqued in brown, black, or mixtures of other dark colors used in your design. Bright or dark shades of red, blue, green, or wood colors can be antiqued with brown, black, or mixtures of other dark colors.

In the list that follows are a few suggested background colors and some of the antiquing shades used over them:

Background Colors:	*Antiquing Colors:*
Bright, medium, or dark shades of red.	Black or brown. (Mix with varnish and turpentine mixture.)
Light or medium shades of green.	Brown or black. (Add yellow or green to the brown shades if desired.)

Shades of coral or salmon.	Alizaran crimson and burnt umber or burnt sienna for a deep shade. A bit of Prussian blue can also be added if desired.
Shades of yellow.	Brown, black, dark blue-green.
Shades of blue.	Brown, black, dark blue-green, or blue-black.
Shades of white, ivory, or off-white.	Yellow-green, blue-green, dusky mauve, shades of brown or black.

Antiquing Furniture and Wood Panels

Whether you are working with stained or painted furniture, the method used for antiquing is the same, as already described. The antiquing color should always be left in the deeper area of carvings, moldings, and ornate designs. Highlights (the wiping off of the antique color) are usually applied to the bulbous portions of turnings, the raised areas of carvings, and the centers of panels. A circular motion is often used to blend the antiquing color on the curved legs and turnings of furniture. The only rule to follow is that of natural wear. Lighten the areas exposed to normal daily wear and deepen the areas likely to have accumulated grime and dirt. The blend should be gradual, from light to dark, and the basic background color should predominate.

All furniture should be finished with two or three coats of varnish to seal and protect the surface. Furniture that may be exposed to heat or water (table tops or outdoor furniture) may be further protected with one or two original coats of a high-gloss, spar-type varnish. To dull the gloss, apply two coats of a semigloss varnish. Waxing the finished surface of furniture, walls, or decorative wood items also gives a pleasing, soft finish. The wax can be either a neutral color or an ordinary paste wax. Apply it in several thin coats, rubbing briskly with a soft cloth between each coat.

LESSON 30

Roses

Painting a shaded rose requires practice to gain complete control of the brush. Through a variety of lessons, you have been practicing all the exercises given in Lesson 1 and putting them to work for you in many designs. You have learned how to fill your brush with two, and then three, shades of paint, and how to apply the brush for clearly shaded strokes. In fact, you have been building a step-by-step foundation for painting the various sections of a rose and have already painted several of these in earlier lessons. Now, putting them all together in your first uncomplicated rose should be a very easy project.

The exercises on lines c and f in Patterns #1 and 2 taught you how to paint the shaded, curved petals of the zinnia lesson, and the rosebud lesson taught you shaded and controlled brush strokes. All that remains to be properly placed are the six petals surrounding the rosebud center. And here you find your old friend, the comma stroke, again doing the work by shading each outside petal.

Before mixing your paint, trace Pattern #35, slip it under your clipboard, and be ready to use it for practice. This may surprise you, but whenever you paint a rose, the pattern serves only as a guide to the size brush you should use and as an aid to producing a balanced arrangement on the object you are decorating. A rose pattern will rarely be painted exactly as it is printed because the pressure you apply to the brush will vary. You may press the brush very firmly and paint each stroke a little larger than the pattern, or you may press lightly and paint the rose a little smaller. In either case, the surrounding leaves or flowers are moved in closer, or out a bit farther, to generally follow the design. A leaf or two, more or less, usually makes no difference in the finished composition.

Brushes

Roses, leaves, and blossoms	Small flat brush
Blossom centers, stems, and leaf	Small pointed brush

Colors

Roses	
Darker shade	Grumbacher red mixed with a bit of cadmium yellow medium, a bit of burnt sienna, and titanium white (similar to swatch #1).
Lighter shade	Titanium white added to some of the above red shade for a pink shade (lighter than swatch #2).
Shading	Red, pink, and white.
Blossoms	Cobalt violet mixed with a bit of Grumbacher red and enough titanium white to match swatch #5, shaded with titanium white.

Blossom centers	Cadmium yellow medium mixed with a bit of titanium white. Accent centers with the darker leaf-green shade.
Leaves	
Darker shade	Permanent green light mixed with a bit of Grumbacher red and enough titanium white to match swatch #38.
Lighter shade	Titanium white, cadmium yellow medium, and raw umber or burnt umber added to some of the above color (similar to swatch #39).
Stems and veins	Raw umber or burnt umber added to a bit of the darker green shade.

Practice Roses

First, use Pattern #35 to practice on, learning all the techniques described below. When you feel you have mastered the rose, mix more paints, trace a clean pattern, and begin painting.

In the diagram, the top two roses show the open and closed construction of the eight-stroke rose. The two bottom roses show the same simple rose, but they also have short comma strokes inside the upper bud section to form a more flared or frilly top. By first painting the top roses with the eight shaded strokes, you will create another stepping stone for painting the additional strokes used in the upper sections of the bottom roses.

Observe the open construction of both rose types. You will see that the rose can be broken into three sections: (1) The upper flared circular petals extending down into the heart of the rose; (2) The middle section, or cup, which encircles the heart and connects with the upper section; (3) The side and lower petals, which connect with the lower area of the half-circular cup.

Photograph #35

Both roses will be shaded just as the rosebud, using a shade of red, a pink shade, and white—all on the brush at one time. To shade the rosebud, you partially filled the brush with the red shade and stroked into the white until a pink shade emerged, leaving an edge of white on the side of the brush for a triple-toned stroke. You may use that method for this rose, too. However, a prettier and more certain shading will result if you mix a separate shade of pink or red.

By now, you have have learned when the paint consistency is just right to produce easily flowing brush strokes, and you can control slightly thicker paint than you could in the early lessons. To paint roses (or other flowers), you will usually be able to use the white paint thicker than the shading colors. A shaded practice stroke will let you quickly see the consistency. If the stroke shows irregular skipped areas, it is too thick and should be thinned slightly. If the paint is too thin, the color will merge with the white and lose the shaded effect.

Now try filling the brush in a different manner, one that will allow you more control over the exact color placement. Stroke into the pink shade until the brush is almost full. Then stroke the right edge of the brush into the white *only twice.* Tip the left corner of the brush into the red shade, and you will be ready to paint with a stroke that is shaded from red to pink to white. Always keep the dark shade inside and the white outside for each stroke.

Remember that the corners of the flat brush are shaping these petals. The upper corner of the flat brush distributes the white in a series of short comma strokes, each slightly below the last one. Two, three, or four short commas can be easily added above and around the deeper red center or heart.

In order to clearly show the white inside strokes, you will need to tip the brush frequently into the white. Since tipping the brush with color adds only a small amount of paint, you will need to pick up more paint frequently. As the comma strokes are completed, you may need to re-accent the red heart by using one corner of the brush to dot in the red or by lightly pivoting the brush in a half circle. After rose is completed, add a few accent dots of white over the red center.

There are two areas of the rose that should always be painted in a deeper shade. These are the center heart of the rose and the lower base of the cup where it joins the outside petals. Keeping these areas darker will give more depth to the rose.

Before painting the six outside petals, study the open and closed rose diagram for a moment. You will notice that the brush has carried the same color placement into the petals—dark to the inside, lighter in the center, and white to the outside. Add both red and white as necessary to separate each added petal. Each of these shaded petals are slightly curved commas and each hugs the rose cup closely as the stroke ends. The inside (or left) corner of the flat brush will guide these strokes into a thin line as the stroke ends.

To start the stroke, lean back on the brush firmly and then lessen the pressure as the stroke begins to curve slightly. As the stroke ends, only the inside corner of the brush will be touching the surface and forming a thin line to end the stroke. Your flat brush should be in tip-top condition to paint these strokes. Bulging, separated ends of the brush will give a fuzzy stroke and will not form a fine line to end the strokes or to smoothly shape the cup and petals.

Complete all the petals on one side before painting the opposite row. In the completed rose, the first upper petal on each side should be even with, or very slightly above, the upper cup line. The second, or middle, petal will be a little shorter, will be a little less curved, and will slightly overlap the first petal as it skims into the base of the cup. And the third lowest petal will be a very short stroke, which will be painted almost horizontally and which will end just under the base of the cup.

As you complete the opposite row of petals, you'll see that the last, short horizontal stroke slightly overlaps the opposite short center stroke. This is just how you want it to look, with only a slight dip separating the two lower petals. Leaves or small flowers will fill in here very nicely. If you have curved the second and third strokes too much, you may have a very pronounced and widespread V. Sometimes you can camouflage this by adding one (or two) short strokes to fill in or, again, by adding leaves or blossoms. Or perhaps you have painted the petals too long and have two on each

Pattern #35

side with room for only one more. If so, just add one more short petal to complete a five-petal rose. It can be very pretty if the petals are placed just right.

For the final touch, smooth and blend in any stray ends of the petal strokes that may have overlapped into the cup area. Pick up a little white on one side of the brush and lightly tip the opposite corner into the red shade. With the white at the top of the brush (outside) and the red below it (inside), take one deep comma stroke around the entire base of the cup. This stroke will smoothly blend and connect the cup and petals and will also distribute additional white around the upper part of the cup. This extra stroke (or two if you need it) may not always be necessary, but use it whenever you feel the cup needs more white or red accent.

There are many ways to construct and paint a rose. As you follow this method, you'll soon learn to add variations and will develop your own style of painting a rose. There is no set right or wrong way to paint a decorative rose. It's right when the results are pleasing.

Roses, rosebuds, and lilacs decorate this metal coal bucket. Basic comma strokes trim inside edges. By Marg Pond.

Lesson Pattern

When you have finished practicing and have arrived at your own style of painting roses, mix more paints, trace a clean Pattern #35, and paint the design according to Photograph #35. When the roses are complete, add the blossoms, leaves, stems, and veins, using the suggested colors.

Rose design on an Early American sewing chest. By Yee Chea Lin.

OPTIONAL LESSON

Roses Painted for Effect

This design allows you to experiment with imaginative rose colors for effect. The colors can be made more pastel with the addition of white and with the use of more white than color on the brush strokes. The upper section of these roses also allows you to try your hand at a more widely flared top. As you paint these frills, flip the brush into quick hairpin curves and concentrate the pressure on the inside corner of the brush.

To paint very small roses on very small objects, you will need a smaller brush (about half the size). This smaller brush will also paint very small blossoms, daisy leaves, and everything that you have painted with the larger brush. In this lesson you have learned three variations, or styles, of painting a small, easy rose.

Use Pattern #36 and Photograph #36 to guide you in painting this design. The suggested colors combined with your own style of painting roses should make for an attractive design perfect for decorating trays, plaques, and other small household items.

Photograph #36

Brushes

Roses, leaves, and blossoms	Small flat brush
Stems, veins, and blossom centers	Small pointed brush

Colors

Roses

Lighter shade	Cobalt violet mixed with alizaran crimson, a bit of Prussian blue, and titanium white (similar to swatch #31).
Darker shade	Titanium white and a bit more alizaran crimson added to some of the above shade (similar to swatch #6).
Third shade	Titanium white.

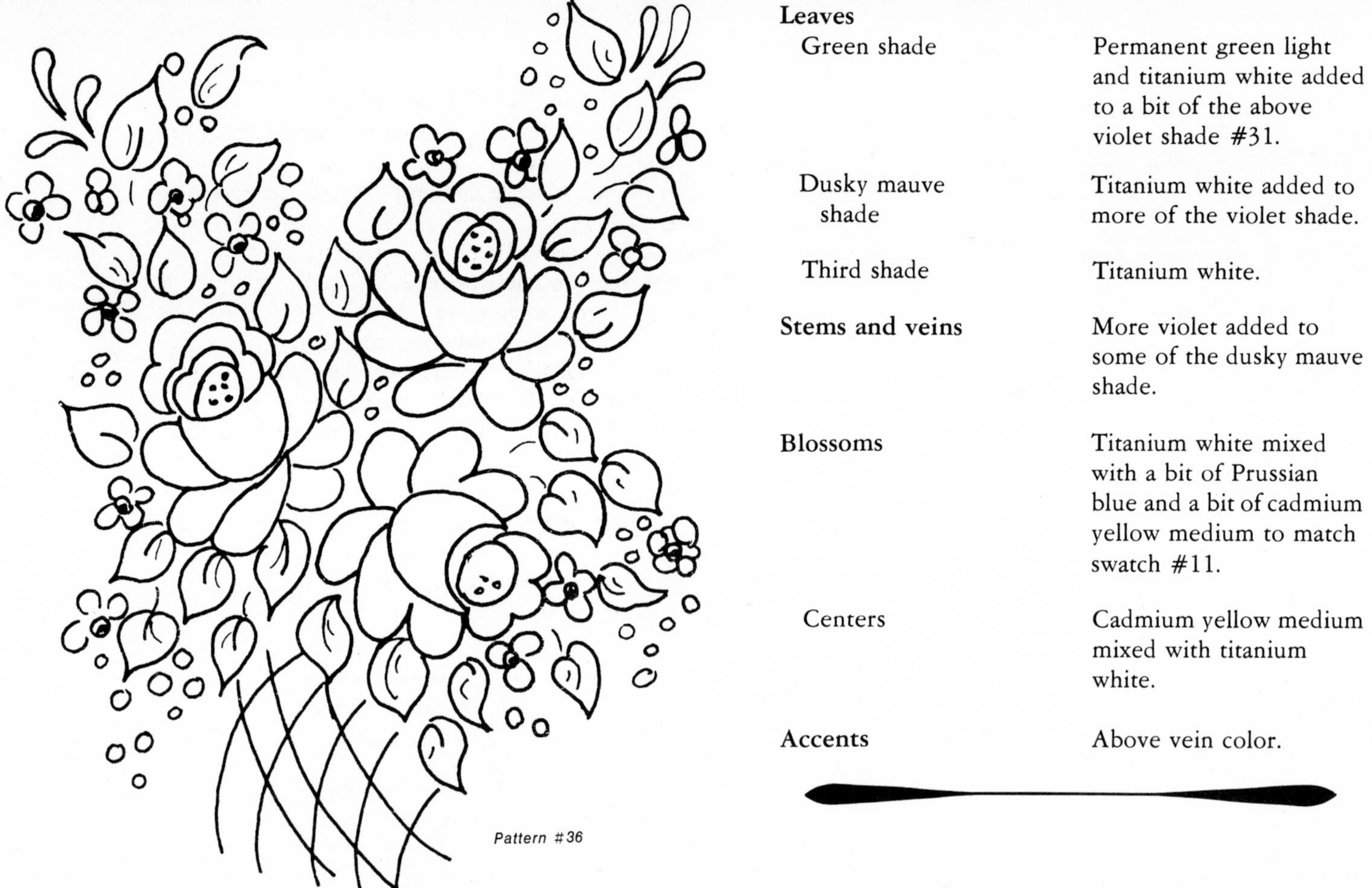

Pattern #36

Leaves	
Green shade	Permanent green light and titanium white added to a bit of the above violet shade #31.
Dusky mauve shade	Titanium white added to more of the violet shade.
Third shade	Titanium white.
Stems and veins	More violet added to some of the dusky mauve shade.
Blossoms	Titanium white mixed with a bit of Prussian blue and a bit of cadmium yellow medium to match swatch #11.
Centers	Cadmium yellow medium mixed with titanium white.
Accents	Above vein color.

LESSON 31

Wood Finishing

Whether you are planning to stain new wood for ornamental objects or new or old wood for furniture, cabinets, or wall panels, it is important to know something about the type and characteristics of the most commonly used woods. Before any wood can be finished with the color and effect you wish to achieve, you must know whether the wood is porous, nonporous, or semiporous. These are of two general types: hardwood and softwood. Hardwood is from broad-leaf trees, is porous, and requires filler. Softwood is from cone-bearing trees, is nonporous, and needs no filler.

All wood is composed of various-sized vessels and membranes forming the substance and grain. After the tree has been cut and planed, the membranes are ruptured, showing lengthwise troughs in the wood. Trees such as walnut, oak, and mahogany (hardwood) have large vessels. To close these pores and to ensure an even stain and finished effect these woods require a filler. Softwood, such as pine, fir, and cedar, has no open vessels and is considered nonporous, requiring no filler before staining. There is also a small group of hardwood (birch, gum, maple, cherry) that contains very small vessels and usually does not require filler. These trees are considered to have a semiporous wood. You may or may not use a thin filler on semiporous wood. It is quite easy to determine the porosity of wood because the open or close grain is visible at a glance. Here is a chart of the most frequently used woods and a guide to whether or not to fill.

Softwood (needs no filler)	Hardwood (needs filler)	Semiporous (needs thin liquid filler)
Pine	Mahogany	Birch
Cedar (red and white)	Walnut	Gum
Fir	Oak	Maple
Cypress	Ash	Cherry
Poplar	Elm	
Willow	Hickory	
Spruce	Satinwood	
	Beech	
	Locust	
	Butternut	

Finishing wood in an endless variety of shades becomes an experience that is challenging and sometimes surprising. It can never become monotonous because of the varying characteristics of the wood itself. After experimenting with several finishes, you will probably want to try your hand at many other stained, pickled, distressed, or novelty effects. You can practice finishing on old or antique furniture and bric-a-brac needing to be restored or on new wood furniture, paneled walls, or decorative wood objects. In any case, there are many modern products that simplify all the methods used to obtain a fine wood finish.

The steps necessary to obtain a professional-looking finished effect, using either new or old wood are as follows:

- Stripping—removing old varnish or paint. Follow by proper sanding.
- Bleaching—lightening the wood, if desired. Follow by proper sanding.
- Sanding—properly preparing the surface for staining.
- Staining—enhancing the wood grain and producing the desired color.
- Filling—producing a smooth, even surface on open-grained wood.
- Finishing coat—sealing and protecting the wood. (Varnish, shellac, or spray fixative is used.)

You will also learn the shorter methods used to stain and finish wood for decorative purposes as well as how to achieve several novelty effects.

Stripping

Before you begin to refinish any piece of old or antique furniture, you first make a careful check for any necessary repairs. Make certain that all joints are tight and that split panels, loose legs, table tops, or drawers are all in good shape. After this is completed, you are ready to take the first step toward the face-lifting and restoration of the furniture.

Stripping is the name given the process for removing old paint or varnish from wood or metal. There are many fine brands of packaged paint and varnish removers for sale in all paint stores, and directions for their proper use are printed on each package or can. Newer, faster, and safer products have been developed in recent years, making stripping a much quicker process than it was in the past. Many of the newer products are of the wash-away type and do not require lengthy scraping with a metal knife. The remover will soften the old finish so that most of it can be washed off with scrub brushes and old rags. Don't rush this process. Let the remover do the work for you. Some furniture will have been given many coats of varnish (or paint) throughout the years, so it is normal to expect to use more than one application of the stripper to completely loosen and remove the old finish.

After the stripping is completed, sand any rough edges or surface areas that may be uneven. (Refer to "Sanding" in this lesson.) If you do not wish to bleach the wood color, omit this step and continue with the final sanding preceding the staining.

Bleaching

Bleaching is the process of lightening the natural wood color with the use of chemically prepared products. It can be used to lighten new wood or to remove some of the stain from the older dark wood. Since the bleaching process is successful only on bare wood, old wood finishes must be removed first by stripping.

Two general types of commercially prepared bleaches can be found in paint and hardware stores. One type of bleach contains two separate solutions and is applied in two separate coats. The second type of bleach also contains two liquids, but they are mixed together immediately before using and applied as one coat. Both types are potent and will produce nearly white tones in all darker woods. Follow the printed directions accompanying the type of bleach you purchase.

Before you apply the bleach, put on a pair of heavy rubber gloves to prevent any chemical irritation to your hands. Avoid splashing the bleach on your clothing, as it can cause fabric to disintegrate. It is generally desirable to lighten the wood a little more than will be wanted for the final finished effect. The stain applied will raise the wood color to the desired shade.

To apply the bleach, use a rag, a synthetic sponge, or a fiber (not bristle) brush. The drying and bleaching time will vary with the type of wood used. If the stain in older wood is quite dark, it may be necessary to apply the bleach several times. After the final bleaching, allow a twelve-hour drying period. The wood must be completely dry before it can be lightly sanded with extra-fine sandpaper. This will remove any chemical residue and also smooth any slight roughness.

Sanding

Whether you are preparing to paint or stain new or old wood, proper sanding is the first step toward a smooth finish. In order to have a smooth, level surface, all rough, scratched, or uneven areas should be sanded with at least two grades of sandpaper: coarse or medium sandpaper to remove deep marks, scratches, or splintered edges; fine or very fine sandpaper to remove scratches left by the coarse sandpaper.

Sometimes people use too coarse a paper for the last sanding, with too much pressure. To avoid this, fold the sandpaper in half with the grits together, and rub them against each other before the final sanding.

Always sand *with* the grain of the wood, not across the grain. Use just enough pressure to remove the deeper scratches, and a very light pressure for the final sanding.

Before painting or staining, always remove the sanding dust by thoroughly cleaning the surface. A tack rag, which can be purchased in all paint stores, is a great aid in dust removal. You may like to make your own tack rag: Dampen a clean, lint-free soft cloth with water. Squeeze lightly and sprinkle generously with turpentine. Add varnish (two or three teaspoonfuls) onto the cloth and squeeze together until almost dry. The added varnish should make the cloth completely damp. If it is stored in an airtight jar or can, it should be usable for some length of time.

To sand large flat areas, use long sweeping strokes *with* the grain of the wood. Sanding *across* the grain will result in only more scratches—with more sanding necessary to remove them.

To sand crevices and grooves, fold the sandpaper into small quarter-sections. Folding the grits together helps keep the sandpaper from slipping and also enables it to fit into the small area more easily.

In addition to sanding before an item is painted or stained, very lightly sand with fine sandpaper between each coat of paint or stain. The first coat of paint or stain will slightly raise the wood grain. Therefore, a slight sanding between coats is necessary to achieve a smooth finish.

Staining Furniture and Walls

If you have not previously stained wood, first follow the method described in the "Staining Wood for Decorative Objects" section farther along in this lesson. Mixing small amounts of the various stain colors will help you plan the finished effects you prefer for furniture or walls. To stain the larger areas of walls and furniture, it's better to purchase the stain color already mixed in quart or pint sizes. You may also mix prepared stains together for a color that is more pleasing to you.

Apply the stain with a bristle brush, using long sweeping strokes with the grain of the wood. Use large rags to wipe off the stain, again wiping *with* the grain. Follow the printed directions on each can of stain for the suggested brushing and wiping process. There are several types of stain on the market, and the directions for the proper use of each may vary slightly.

It is common to find light or dark streaks in the same piece of wood or to find that a piece of furniture is constructed of more than one type of wood. It is a safe practice to wipe off the stain very quickly so that it does not penetrate the light areas too deeply. Apply additional stain to the streaked area, allowing it to stand longer and penetrate more deeply before wiping. If the stain color is too dark, some of it can be removed by wiping with turpentine.

You may choose to mix the stain and filler together for a single application, thus saving a step. This time-saver is often used, and the final results are just as pleasing. If the stain and filler are applied together, you will save another step by eliminating the need for a separate seal coat for the stain and for the filler.

Wood Filler

Wood filler, which can be found in all paint and hardware stores, is made in both paste and liquid form. It usually requires a twelve-hour drying time unless it is a fast-drying type, which needs only three to four hours. Read the label and directions carefully. Wood filler is made in all natural wood colors and in a light transparent color suitable for light wood finishes. The natural (or transparent) color can easily be mixed with a small amount of oil stain or oil color to produce any shade you wish. You may like to try this quicker method, mixing some of the stain color with the filler. Directions for mixing the stain and filler together are printed on the can of filler.

Detailed directions for thinning the paste form of filler are printed on each can. The filler is generally thinned with small amounts of turpentine used a little at a time until it is of brushing consistency.

With a fairly stiff brush, brush the filler lengthwise so that it is packed into the pores. In a short time (ten to fifteen minutes), the filler will begin to show dull areas. You will need a large coarse rag—rolled into a pad—to rub more of the filler into the pores of the wood before it is completely dry. Remove any surplus filler by rubbing across the grain, and finish by wiping with clean rags, stroking *with* the grain. One note of caution: After the filler has hardened, it is very difficult to remove. Plan to cover only the areas that you will be able to wipe before the filler is dry. (A cloth dampened in turpentine may help soften the filler if it has become too hard.) The filler must be allowed to dry completely before sanding with very fine sandpaper.

Whether or not to seal the filler is a matter of personal preference. The same is true of sealing the stain coat before applying the filler. An expert craftsman would choose to seal both the filler and the stain coat to produce first-quality work.

The sealer is usually a four-pound, cut, white shellac, which has been thinned about 40 percent with alcohol. Two coats of the sealer should be applied, allowing two hours' drying time after the final coat. The thinned shellac will produce a soft surface for easier light sanding with 6/0 sandpaper. This sanding should be especially light so that you do not sand holes into the seal coat. After this is completed, use the tack rag to remove the dust and sand particles.

Finishing Coat for Furniture and Walls

To enhance the grain and to seal the wood, two or more coats of varnish are usually applied. Shellac may also be used but is considered less durable than varnish. Varnish is made in two finishes—a satin and a high-gloss. Before applying the varnish, make certain that the surface is free of dust by wiping it with a tack rag. The varnish will magnify any dust particles and will even catch dust from the air. If possible, keep your work free from moving air.

Varnish should be used just as it comes from the can. However, it is usually recommended that you pour the amount of varnish you expect to use at one time into a clean container. Reseal the can of varnish to keep it clean and free of dust particles. Discard any unused varnish—never pour it back into the clean can of varnish. Do not unduly stir the varnish in the container. This will cause air bubbles to form, which will be carried by the brush onto the surface.

A good-quality brush, whether pure bristle or synthetic, may be used to apply the varnish. A chiseled-edged brush is preferable, and a popular width is about $2\frac{1}{2}$ inches wide. When applying the varnish, stroke *with* the grain of the wood and use only enough varnish to cover the area. Flat surfaces are varnished from one outside edge across to the opposite edge, brushing well to evenly distribute the varnish. Chair rungs and round turnings can more easily be brushed round and round and then lightly cross-brushed with just the tip of the brush to finish the work.

Allow the varnish to dry twenty-four hours between coats and after the final coat. Any slight roughness on the dry surface will be due to dust. These can be removed by using 6/0 steel wool. Use the pad of steel wool to stroke *with* the wood grain. Use only enough pressure to smooth the surface.

Waxing the finished surface of furniture or walls will enrich the wood color and give a pleasing, soft effect. The wax can be either a neutral color or ordinary paste wax. It is better to apply the wax in several thin coats rather than in one heavy coat, rubbing briskly with a soft clean cloth between each coat. Wood or metal that is to be used outdoors may be brushed or sprayed with a tough heat- and water-resistant varnish. This will have a high gloss but will dull through weathering. If you don't want to wait for the weather to do this work, just apply two coats of low-gloss varnish over the high gloss.

Staining Wood for Decorative Objects

Since decorated wood objects are not usually subjected to the daily rigors of household wear, they can be attractively finished in a minimum of time. Because of this, the staining and finishing of wood to be used for decorative purposes usually requires less effort in the finishing details.

Pine, or any other softwood, is used almost exclusively for hand-painted objects. Because softwoods do not require filling they can be sanded smooth and stained immediately. Any of the softwoods are less expensive than the hardwoods. They can be purchased in several grades, the price varying with the quality. First grade, clearly, is more costly. Second-grade wood has occasional knotholes, is less perfect, and is less expensive. For many decorators, an occasional knothole adds interest to the object, provided that the design is not painted directly over it. It is frequently possible to cut around and discard any objectionable areas found in the second-grade panel.

As you have just read, the first step in preparing any wood for the stain coat is sanding. Sanding can produce several effects. If you want the wood object to have a fine, smooth finish, do the final sanding with very fine sandpaper. Sand *with* the grain of the wood, and use more pressure to cause deeper grooves on the outer areas. Sand down the square corners to rounded ones for an added appearance of age.

If you would like to distress the wood even more, here are several suggestions. Deep scratches and marks can be added by using an ice pick to punch imitation worm holes or long irregular scratches; striking the wood repeatedly with heavy metal keys or chain; using a metal file to chisel long grooves along the side.

Use smaller wood panels for your first practice staining. The stain may be applied on smaller wood objects with either a small cloth saturated with the stain or a small, inexpensive bristle brush. Cover the wood thoroughly and immediately wipe it off with a lint-free rag. If the stain is not quickly removed, it may penetrate too deeply and become darker than you wish. If the color is not as deep as you want, apply another stain coat and wait a little longer before wiping and blending with the rag. Remember that you can always add antiquing over any stain color to deepen it.

After staining the wood surface, allow about ten or fifteen minutes' drying time before using a light coat of the quick-drying spray fixative. The fixative not only dries the stain more quickly but also acts as a thin seal coat. Varnish or shellac, which has been thinned, may also be brushed on the wood surface as a seal coat. If either of these are used, the stain must be thoroughly dry before applying the sealer. The brushed-on seal coats will also require a longer drying period.

Wood stains can be purchased in many colors and can be mixed with the color stains to produce an endless variety. Or, you may want to mix your own color stains. A container for the stain can be made by folding a piece of aluminum foil to make a dish, or you can use a small, disposable, aluminum baking dish. Mixing a color stain is simple. Just squeeze tube oil colors into the foil container, adding small amounts of turpentine. Use your spatula to dissolve and combine the oil color with the turpentine until the mixture is smooth and of a watery consistency. Before applying the stain to the object, test the color on the underside. If it is too dark, add more turpentine or a little white to dilute. If it is too light, add more tube oil to deepen. It is better to keep the first stain color a little on the light side. You can always give another application to deepen it, or you can use an additional, deeper shade of antiquing.

The following are a few of the more frequently used stain colors, which can also be mixed in small amounts.

- Any of the brown wood shades can be produced by mixing burnt umber with titanium white or yellow to lighten. Add raw umber or ivory black to deepen. Burnt sienna can be added for a red-brown effect. Thin with turpentine.
- Light, medium, or dark green stain can be made by using permanent green light mixed with raw umber or burnt umber to deepen or titanium white to lighten. Add viridian green when a blue-green is desired. Add a little red to the green shades if desired. Thin with turpentine.
- Yellow-green can be made by mixing cadmium yellow medium with permanent green light. Use raw umber to deepen. Thin with turpentine.
- Yellow-brown can be made by mixing cadmium yellow medium with burnt umber or burnt sienna. Add raw umber or ivory black to deepen. Thin with turpentine.
- Dark red can be made by mixing Grumbacher red with raw umber or ivory black to deepen. Thin with turpentine.

All stained wood can be deepened further by lightly antiquing in shades of darker or lighter brown. The outside areas are usually darkened more heavily, with a lighter effect around the decorated area. Apply the stain with a brush or a rag, and quickly wipe with a clean rag. Since this will penetrate and dry quickly, apply only on small areas at a time.

To transfer a design to a finished panel or object, center and tape the tracing paper in place. If the wood is dark, you will need to use colored carbon paper (white or yellow can be more easily seen). Dressmaker carbon, which can be found in dime stores, comes in a packet of assorted colors. Slip the carbon under the taped design, and trace the outlines with the fine wood end of your small pointed brush or an empty ballpoint pen. Remove the pattern, and you are ready to paint.

Novelty Effects

A great variety of colored-wood effects can be achieved by using a light-colored filler or a light-colored flat paint over a darker-colored stain. These effects, often called limed, pickled, or frosted, are widely used on paneled walls, furniture, and bric-a-brac. They are more frequently used on open-grained wood (such as oak, chestnut, mahogany) but may also be used on close-grained wood (such as pine and birch). Both open- and close-grained woods will have been previously stained in your choice of color—green, blue, gray, or any of the wood colors.

For close-grained wood (needing no filler), first sand and smooth the surface. Wipe clean with a tack rag. Brush on a coat of any flat undercoat paint and immediately wipe off with a soft cloth. Wipe *across* the grain to remove the excess paint and to force it into the wood grain. Use a fresh cloth to finish blending and wipe *with* the grain to complete the work. This will leave a thin, white deposit in the grain of the wood, which produces the limed, pickled, or frosted effect.

When completely dry, seal the wood with a thin coat of white shellac. Let this dry thoroughly, and sand lightly before applying the finish coat. The final finish may be of varnish, either gloss or satin. On decorative items not subjected to the rigors of daily use, the spray fixative will be sufficient to seal on the effect.

You can save one step with open-grained wood (needing a filler) by thinning the wood filler with a light-colored oil stain or flat undercoat paint mixed together until of brushing consistency. The light deposit that it will leave in the pores of the wood will produce the limed, or pickled, effect. Use a soft cloth to wipe and blend the mixture if necessary. When this is dry, lightly sand the surface and remove the sanding dust with a tack rag. Finish the surface with either satin or gloss varnish or with a spray fixative.

Spattering

Spattering the painted, stained, or antiqued surface with fine specks of dark paint or India ink is a technique you can try for variety. It was once used to suggest worm holes in antique reproductions, but in recent years it has been widely used on more expensive traditional furniture and bric-a-brac. While it is not a difficult skill to learn, it may take a little practice to get just the right amount of spatter where you want it. For this reason, always spatter on a completely dry surface so that any unpleasing results can be easily removed. Spread newspaper over your work area to catch any stray specks. You will need a coarse, stiff-bristle brush to hold the dark paint or ink and your spatula to flip the brush edge sharply and spatter over the object. If you are spattering furniture or large objects, you will need to use a much wider stiff brush (such as a wallpaper-paste brush) and a longer stick or board to flip the paint.

Begin by using black or brown India ink. It is not only attractive and easy to use, but it is also the perfect consistency for spattering. Later, it will be a guide as to how thin you should mix your tube paints for spattering.

Black or dark brown paint is also used for the spattering, but any dark color is effective. Use either turpentine or the antiquing mixture to dissolve the dark paint. If the paint consistency is a little thick (similar to the antique mixture), the spattering will be more effective and will not appear as watery blobs. Fill only the edges of the brush with the paint to avoid spattering in heavy deposits.

Spattering is also used for wall or floor decoration. Two or three colors are loaded on the large brush and flipped over the surface. The paint used can be of any type and should be thinned very little. A novel effect can be achieved by using a wide brush to lightly spread these colors together (in one direction) after the paint is slightly set.

Another handsome effect can be created by using artists' gold oil color (Malfa gold, by Weber). This is thinned to a flowing consistency with turpentine and lightly blended over the antiquing color. Usually applied to the outside areas of decorative items, it can be streaked lightly with the small bristle brush or smoothly blended with a soft cloth or the fingertips. Hand-rubbing the gold over an antiqued surface will produce a most attractive faint shimmer of old gold. This is especially effective on furniture or bric-a-brac with raised carvings or turnings.

Don't be afraid of color. Plunge right in and experiment with several different colors, one right over another, and you will be happily surprised at the results. You can always blend additional colors until the results are pleasing to you. And don't forget to finish the back or underside of the object. These unseen areas are a good place to begin the antiquing, allowing you to experiment with shadings and effects.

The subtle blendings of the many colors used for antiquing is an art. No commercially prepared product will produce the pleasing variety of shades you can achieve with your own mixture of colors and creativity.

LESSON 32

Soldiers and Drums

Soldiers' uniforms may be painted in many different color combinations, ranging from somewhat authentic colorings to purely imaginative shadings. After painting this lesson, you may want to paint uniforms in brighter or deeper shades of blue or red. Interchange the coat and trouser colors to contrast with ivory, beige, or brown shades. To match fabrics and wallpapers, paint the soldier and drum in some of the brighter combinations of blue and green, coral, brown and chartreuse, yellow-green shades of pale blue with deeper blue, green, or wine shades. Among all the colors mixed from your swatch chart, there is an endless variety of color combinations to guide you in selecting and planning each new design.

Brushes

Entire soldier and drum	Small flat brush
All fine detail	Small pointed brush

Colors

Face	
Flesh tone (face and hands)	Titanium white mixed with a bit of burnt sienna to match swatch #60.
Deeper shading	Burnt sienna, thinned slightly with turpentine.
Cheeks	Grumbacher red thinned with turpentine.
Lips	Grumbacher red mixed with burnt umber or burnt sienna, thinned with turpentine.
Trousers	
Undercoat	Burnt umber mixed with titanium white (similar to swatch #53), thinned slightly with turpentine.
Deeper shading	Burnt umber, thinned slightly with turpentine.
Lighter shading	Titanium white.
Drum	
Drum head (lower side)	Cadmium yellow medium mixed with burnt umber (similar to swatch #47).
Drum body	Burnt umber mixed with some of the above shade #53 (similar to swatch #51), thinned slightly with turpentine.
Center highlight	Titanium white or pale yellow.
Deeper accent	Raw umber or a mixture of raw umber and burnt umber, thinned slightly with turpentine.
Drum band, cords, sticks, pocket, cuffs, and buttons	Above shade #47.

Coat and hat	Prussian blue mixed with raw umber or ivory black and titanium white for a navy blue shade.
Dark shadows	Raw umber or ivory black, thinned slightly with turpentine.
Lighten	Titanium white.
Red trim	Grumbacher red, thinned slightly with turpentine.
Deeper shading	Raw umber or ivory black.
Boots	
Undercoat	Ivory black mixed with titanium white for a medium or dark charcoal shade, thinned slightly with turpentine.
Deeper shading	Ivory black, thinned slightly with turpentine.
Lighten	Titanium white.
Hair	Titanium white added to some of above coat shade for a light slate blue.
Deepen and accent	Above shade mixed with more of the coat shade to deepen slightly.
Lighten and highlight	Titanium white.

Photograph #37

Pattern #37

Lesson Pattern

Face and Hands

Before painting the face and hands of the soldier in Pattern #37, outline them in pen and ink. The entire figure should also be outlined, using either the graphite paper on a light background, colored dressmaker's carbon on a dark background, or the pen and ink. All the colors used in this design will easily cover the traced outline, but you will need a faint outline to follow for the proper placement of the features and the hairline.

Using the small flat brush, block in the face and hand areas with the flesh tone. The shading and detail of the face and hands may be added now or later. You may decide to wait until these areas are dry before completing this step, as it is much easier to remove any mistakes then. Use the spray fixative if you wish to hasten the drying time.

To accent the area under the ear and into the jaw, use the small pointed brush and a very small amount of thinned burnt sienna to make a light L stroke. Dry-brush this color lightly, and blend it into the flesh color. Use a small amount of the same color to deepen slightly the back of the neck, the upper forehead, and the base of the nose. When this is completed, use only the tip of the small pointed brush and thin dark paint to outline the eyebrow. Then add the eye.

Dry-brush a bit of the deeper color around the nose and upper lip. Add only a bit of dark red over the lips. Use almost a dry brush and bit of Grumbacher red to add a suggestion of color to the cheeks.

Use the small pointed brush and thin dark paint to accent the hands and fingers. Lightly dry-brush if necessary, and add white highlights over the center of the hands.

Trousers

The small brush is used to paint the trousers in the suggested light tan shade #53. Wipe the brush before adding a little of the slightly thinned burnt umber to one corner of it. Use this color to deepen the rear leg. Use the same color on one corner of the brush to deepen the entire right and left outside trouser line and above the boots. Add a little white to the center leg area, and wipe the brush before lightly dry-brushing the lighter center area into the deeper outside shading. Use the corner of the flat brush or the small pointed brush to add a few wrinkles in the trousers at the knee and above the boot. If needed, lightly dry-brush for a soft blending.

Drum

Use the small flat brush and the yellow shade #47 to paint the inside center of the drum head. When this is completed, add a small white highlight to the center area and dry-brush lightly.

Clean the brush and use the brown shade #51 to paint the entire drum body. When this is completed, add white or pale yellow to the center area. Lightly whisk the brush across this area for a light blending.

Clean the brush, fill it with the yellow shade #47, and paint the upper and lower bands of the drum. When this is completed, use the small pointed brush and thin dark brown paint to add a fine line around the inside of the drum head and above and below both bands. Wipe the brush, and blend a little of the brown into the yellow shade used for the bands.

When the drum is dry, use the small pointed brush to paint the cords in the deeper yellow shade. Add darker or lighter accent lines beside this color if desired. Use the same yellow shade #47 to paint the drumsticks, accenting the side or center with a fine line of white or pale yellow.

Coat and Hat

With the small flat brush, paint the blue coat and hat next. The shade of blue may be brighter than that shown in the photograph if you choose.

Fill the brush with the blue shade and block in the entire coat. As you paint the sleeve, keep just inside the outline to separate the body and arm more easily for shading later. When this is completed, wipe the brush and add only a little of the slightly thinned raw umber or ivory black to about one-fourth of the brush width. Add this color over the blue to suggest shadows along the coat front, across the right shoulder-curve and into the elbow, the left coat area under the arm, and along the upper back of the coat.

Use a very small amount of the brown or black to brush the color up from the cuff, lower right arm, and slightly above the red coat lining. Wipe the brush before lightly dry-brushing and blending the edge of the two coats together.

Wipe the brush thoroughly before adding a little white to one side of the brush. Paint a small line of white on the coat and in front of the upper right side of the arm, along the entire lower left side of the arm, and into the center coat area. Wipe the brush frequently as the white is added and as the white is dry-brushed to blend light areas against dark areas for contrast.

Now paint the hat, using the same blue and either brown or black to deepen the lower side and front. Add white across the crown and blend into the blue shade.

Paint the red cuffs, collar, and coat lining now, even though the blue is still damp. The red pocket and yellow detail of the cuffs and pocket must be added after the "under" colors are dry.

Red Trim and Boots

Using the small flat brush, fill in the coat lining with Grumbacher red. Wipe the brush before adding a small amount of black or brown to one corner. Use this color along the lower side of the red lining, lightly dry-brushing up into the red for a deeper shadow effect.

Paint the collar and cuffs with the same red, and lightly dry-brush with a bit of brown or black.

Undercoat the boots with the charcoal shade, using the small flat brush. Use the small pointed brush and thin black paint to accent the front of the toes, along the lower foot, and the entire heel. Use either the small pointed brush or the corner of the flat brush to add a little black to the front and back of each boot. Lightly dry-brush the black into the boot center. Add a little white to the center of the boot, and lightly whisk the brush *across* for a slightly streaked highlight.

Hair and Finishing Touches

Paint the hair with the small pointed brush, using a very light slate blue. Use white to paint a fine line across the top of the round curl and to highlight the back of the tied hair. Accent the lower side of the round curl with a slightly deeper shade of slate blue. Use the small pointed brush to add fine curved lines of the lighter slate blue over the round curl. Accent with a few curved white lines. Slightly deepen the lower hairline and into the tied hair. The bow is painted in the blue of the coat collar.

The small section of the drum strap is shaded in the same colors used for the hair.

Paint the red pocket and the yellow detail of the coat cuffs and pockets after the coat color is dry.

LESSON 33

Federal Design: The Eagle

The eagle and other federal designs have become a prominent feature of early American decor. These emblems are used not only for numerous hand-decorated items but also in wallpaper designs, curtain and drapery fabrics, and ornamental brass and metal objects.

The decorative eagle in Pattern #38 can be shaded in a variety of brown colorings, or you can copy the shadings of old tavern and inn signs showing the eagle in shades of dark red, blue-gray, gold, or black and white. Feel free to exercise your artistic license, and paint the eagle in any shades you prefer.

Paint the eagle with a flat or a pointed brush, whichever is easier and creates the feathered effect you prefer. You may even want to use both brushes for the same eagle. The large pointed brush will hold more paint than the flat brush, allowing you to take more strokes before refilling. For this reason, use the large pointed brush whenever you are painting very large eagles and the flat brush to paint smaller eagles. Either brush will shape the feathered wings in almost the same way. Experiment with both brushes and see the similarity of the strokes.

Before mixing the shades of brown for the eagle's wings, use the pen and drawing ink to trace in the eye and brow line. This will show through the white paint enough for you to later paint the eye in the proper space.

Brushes

Eagle wings and body feathers	Small flat or large pointed brush

Beak and eye, fine detail on wings, claws, and branch	Small pointed brush
Leaves and berries	Small flat brush

Colors

Wings	
(A) Deepest shade	Raw umber, softened with turpentine.
(B) Lower outside feathers	Burnt sienna mixed with a bit of cadmium yellow medium and a bit of burnt umber (deeper than swatch #58). Edge inside (toward body) feather strokes with a bit of titanium white.
(C) Second row of feathers	More burnt umber added to some of the above shade (deeper than swatch #51). Edge inside feather strokes with a bit of titanium white.
(D) Third row of feathers	More raw umber added to some of the above shade. Edge inside feather strokes with titanium white.
(E and F) Outside upper neck and lower tail feathers	Titanium white added to some of color C (similar to swatch #52), shaded with titanium white.
(G and H) Body and legs	Bit of titanium white mixed with some of shade #51, re-accented with dark brown.
(I and J) Head and neck feathers and top of wing	Titanium white, dry-brushed with a bit of brown for an off-white shading.
Eye	Cadmium yellow medium mixed with a bit of raw umber and a bit of titanium white.
Dark detail	Raw umber mixed with burnt umber or ivory black, thinned with turpentine.
Beak and feet	Cadmium yellow medium mixed with a bit of burnt sienna and a bit of titanium white to match swatch #44.
Lighten	Titanium white.
Darken	Burnt umber mixed with a little of the above yellow shade for a darker contrast.
Claws	Dark brown used for eye detail or ivory black.
Leaves	Any light and darker shade of green.
Berries	Cadmium red light or Grumbacher red shaded with brown or white.

Pattern #38

Lesson Pattern

Wings

Paint the wings for this lesson with the small flat brush. (The large pointed brush may also be used for this size of wing but with a light pressure.) Notice that each row of wing feathers is slanted in toward the head of the eagle. It's easier to slant the left wing with the clipboard turned upside down or to the side. Using the deepest shade of brown (A under *Colors*) in your brush, begin to paint the right wing, painting a thin line along the lower curve of the wing (part A on Pattern #38). Add more paint to the brush, and use short press-strokes to fill in this area more heavily. Follow the short lines on the pattern, and slant the dark press-strokes about one-fourth inch into the wing area. This will look dark and ragged, but let it wait until the uneven edges are later covered with feathers. The upper dark area will remain untouched, suggesting a dark shadow in the wing.

Clean the brush and fill it with the red-brown shade (B under *Colors*). Slide the right side of the brush into the edge of white, adding only an edge of white to the brush. Begin to paint the longer outside row of feathers from the top of the wing down into the shorter feathers joining the body (part B on Pattern #38). Keep the brown shade to the upper side of the brush and the white below it for each feather stroke. By tipping the brush slightly to the left, each feather will have a rounded tip. Use the inside corner of the flat brush to guide and shape each stroke. Don't worry about following the exact outline of each feather. Just follow the general shape of the wing, and let your brush width be your yardstick for the size of each feather. A few feathers more or less will make no difference in the finished effect.

You will need to add both brown and white for each feather. Be sure that the paint is not too thick so that you have an easily flowing stroke.

The second row of feathers (part C on the pattern) will be painted in the same manner, using the slightly deeper brown shade (shade C under *Colors*) on the brush with an edging of white below it. As each additional row of feathers is added, be sure to overlap the underlying row of feathers slightly. Paint the third row of feathers (part D under *Colors* and on the pattern) with very short strokes and shade with the deeper brown and white. End the short strokes just under the deep brown accent that is part A on the pattern outline.

Now repeat the whole procedure to complete the left wing.

Neck

The various shaded sections of the eagle are ready to be painted now. Clean the brush in turpentine and lift aside a small amount of shade #51 (C), adding white until it is as light as shade #52. Fill the brush with the lighter brown, and begin to fill in area E on the pattern. Place the brush flat against the unpainted, upper, outside wing-line, and end each stroke just under the irregular outline of the neck feathers. End the short strokes of light brown at the curve of the upper wing. Wipe the brush and pick up a little white while dry-brushing a white highlight along the outside of the neck and lightly over the remaining brown.

Body and Legs

Before shading the body (H) and legs (G), use the deepest brown (A) to outline the upper curve of the leg with short press-strokes. This is a temporary shading line to help separate the body from the leg. Clean the brush and fill with brown shade #51 (C). Beginning under the line of neck feathers near the outside curved wing outline, use the narrow side of the brush to paint overlapping short feather strokes.

Undercoat the entire body with the flat brush, tipping it slightly to the side to form teardrop feathers on the legs just under the deeper shade A. When this is completed, clean the brush and fill it with the deeper brown shade (D). A little white may be added to the side of the brush as a second application of teardrop feathers is painted over the still-wet undercoat. This final body feathering should be painted lightly and at random for a softly shaded effect.

Photograph #38

Wipe the brush and lightly blend the dark curve of the leg into the brown shades. Highlight the top of the leg with a bit of white.

Lower Tail Feathers

Paint the tail feathers in the lighter brown shade used for the neck (E). Stroke the feathers from the outside into the shaded body. Wipe the brush and add a small amount of white, brushing over the brown color to form shaded feathers. When this is completed, wipe the brush and lightly dry-brush a little of the darker body color into the lighter tail feathers.

Wing Detail

Add the finishing detail of the upper curved wing (area J) now that the body is completed. Mix a bit of the brown shade (C) with white for a deep off-white color. Fill the brush half or more with the brown shade (C), and add the off-white to the opposite side of the brush. Following the outline of the wing detail, begin the stroke at the body line while keeping the off-white at the top of the brush and the brown below it. This will not be one continuous stroke but a series of three or four connected shorter strokes ending in a pointed line over the outstretched wing. Be certain that the paint is just thin enough to flow easily and still cover well.

After both wings are completed, wipe the brush and pick up a little of the deeper brown shade (A). Use very short press-strokes to re-accent the original dark color, and brush the brown lightly here and there into the lower area of the wing detail just painted. If necessary, add a few dark feathers around the wing as it joins the body. Look over the wing and body shading to see whether there is a need for a dark or lighter accent before the paint is dry. Frequently a few thin lines of very dark brown or black paint are slipped in beside a few outside feathers for additional contrast. Use the small pointed brush and very thin paint for this detail.

Eagle Head and Neck

Paint the top of the head (area I) with white, and shade into an off-white for the remainder of the head and neck feathers. Turn the pattern, if necessary, and paint the off-white feathers in short teardrop brush strokes. As you brush into the brown body shades, the brush will pick up a little of the darker color. Let this bit of color remain in your brush because it helps the shading. Paint the last row of neck feathers from the inside down so that the feathers have an irregular or ragged ending.

Eye

Before painting the eye, use a small amount of a brown shade to dry-brush a faint shadow around the white area connecting the beak. Use the small pointed brush to fill in the outside semicircle with the yellow shade.

Outline the yellow with dark brown or black. Paint a small half-circle of the dark color for the eye, adding a small white highlight in the center. Use the same dark thin paint to add the curving brow line over the eye. For a fierce-looking eagle, you will need to paint only a little more than half an eye with the curved brow obscuring the remainder of the eye.

Beak

The beak can be painted most easily with a pointed brush. Use the lighter yellow shade #44 to paint the upper half of the beak and the slightly deeper shade for the lower half. Deepen the open area of the mouth with a bit of light brown. Dry-brush a bit of this color over the lower beak and along the white feathers near the beak. Add a bit of white over the top of the beak, and blend it into the yellow shade.

Feet and Claws

Using the small pointed brush, paint the feet with the lighter yellow. Use the deeper yellow to darken the inside of the feet, to add fine lines of thin brown paint across the feet, and to outline if necessary.

Use thin dark brown or black paint to fill in the curved claws.

Branch and Leaves

Before painting the leaves, use the small pointed brush to paint the branch in a deeper green or a brown-green shade. Then, use the small flat brush to paint the leaves in any two shades of green you may choose.

Early American wooden box decorated with eagles, bunting, and rosebuds. Early nineteenth century. Courtesy New York Historical Society, New York City.

OPTIONAL PATTERN

Federal Design: The Flag and Horn

The draped flag, shields, and crests are an important feature of many federal designs. Painting the flag used in Pattern #39 will also enable you to paint a shield easily whenever it is a part of other designs.

Here, again, use the pen and ink to outline the inside of the flag stripes. Don't outline the entire flag, however, since the ink will show through.

Brushes

Flag	Small flat brush
Stars, horn, and tassel detail	Small pointed brush
Horn and cord	Large pointed brush

Colors

Blue field	Prussian blue mixed with a bit of ivory black and a bit of titanium white (lighter than swatch #7).
White stripes and stars	Titanium white.
Shading color	Titanium white added to above blue shade for a medium blue-gray shade.
Red stripes	Grumbacher red, thinned with turpentine.
Shading color	Burnt umber, softened in turpentine.
Horn	Cadmium yellow medium mixed with a bit of burnt sienna and titanium white (similar to swatch #44 or #47).
Shading color	Burnt umber, softened in turpentine.

Lesson Pattern

The beginning point in this design is the blue field of the flag. Use the small flat brush and the blue shade to outline and fill in this area.

White Stripes

Paint the center stripe at the top of the flag first, painting the lower stripes from left to right, or the reverse if you choose. With the brush filled with white, square the end of the stripe by running the brush across the end. Resume painting the stripe from top to bottom and from right to left.

You may need two or three strokes of white to cover the background color. Before adding the final stroke to complete the stripe, stroke into the deeper shade of blue-gray or light charcoal, blending it on the left side of the stripe with the deeper color and blending it into the white. If the shading color does not have enough contrast, deepen the blue-gray or charcoal a little more and lightly dry-brush over the shaded area. Additional shading may be lightly dry-brushed even after the design is completely dry.

Paint and shade the remaining white stripes in the same manner. Here the white should be allowed to dry, or, if you wish, you may spray it dry. When the white is entirely dry, the red of the adjoining stripes will not become pink as they merge. To be safe, either spray it or put it aside to dry.

Photograph #39

Red Stripes

Paint and shade the red stripes in the same manner, using Grumbacher red for the brighter shade and thin burnt umber for the deeper red accent. (Thin black or very dark blue could also be used to shade the red stripes.) If you are using the spray fixative, give the entire design several light coats to hasten the drying time of the red shades.

Horn, Cord, and Tassel

The horn, cord, and tassel may be added while the red is still wet, but proceed with caution.

The horn will be more easily painted with a pointed brush, though others of larger size could be painted with a flat brush. Use the deep yellow shade to fill in the entire horn. When finished, wipe the brush before adding a little of the thinned burnt umber to the tip of the pointed brush and painting the open end of the horn. Continue the brown line along the underside of the entire horn. Wipe the brush and use only the tip to blend and dry-brush the brown into the yellow along the lower side and slightly over the horn.

Using the yellow shade, paint the tassel. Add thin lines of brown for a fringed effect. Add one or two white highlights if desired.

Use the spray again to set the horn colors before painting the cord. Use the tip of the pointed brush with white to paint the cord. Wipe the brush and add a little of the gray-blue or charcoal to the brush tip, blending the deeper shade along the cord's underside.

Stars

Add the stars when the blue is dry. Use the white and the small pointed brush to paint these freehand. An easy way to paint the stars is to paint an **A**, crossing the **A** a little higher and longer than usual and then joining the crossbar with each leg.

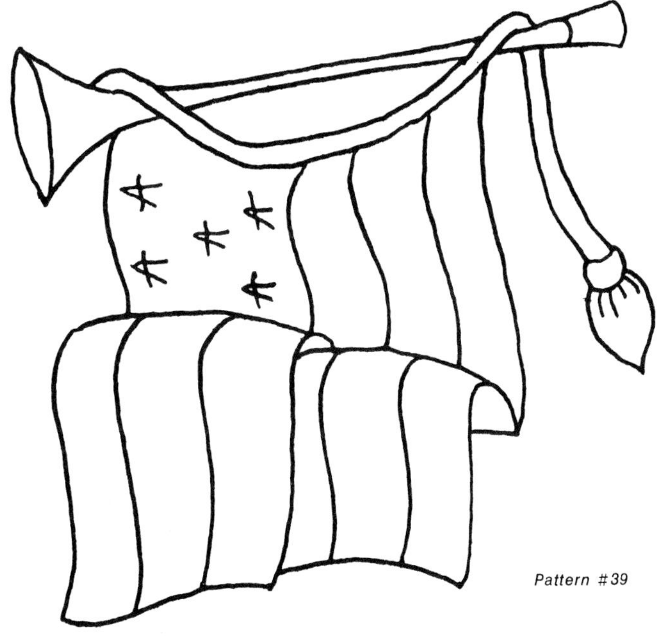
Pattern #39

Photograph #40

LESSON 34

Vegetable Basket

Perhaps you should save this design for a rainy day since it will take more than two hours to complete. Many of the colors are repeated in the shading of several vegetables and are lightened or deepened for more contrast. If you will read the lesson before mixing the paint, you will be able to more accurately gauge the amount of paint needed. Remember, too, that any unthinned paint will remain moist and usable for several days if it is covered. Just place a sheet of waxed paper over the glass or disposable palette when you are finished painting. This is an airtight seal—any paint adhering to it can be lifted with the spatula and replaced on the palette.

Brushes

Basket, larger vegetables, and leaves	Large flat brush
Small vegetables and leaves	Small flat brush
All fine detail	Small pointed brush
Corn husks	Large pointed brush

Colors

Basket	
Inside shadow and accent lines over basket slats	Cadmium yellow medium mixed with a bit of burnt umber and enough titanium white to match swatch #45.
Outside undercoat	Cadmium yellow medium mixed with a bit of burnt sienna and titanium white (deeper than swatch #49), thinned slightly with turpentine.
Deepen	A bit of cadmium yellow medium mixed with cadmium red light (similar to swatch #48), thinned slightly with turpentine.
Lighten	A bit of ivory black added to some of the above shade (similar to swatch #50).
Woven slat accents	Shadow shade #45, thinned slightly with turpentine.
Squash (or gourd)	
Undercoat	Titanium white mixed with burnt sienna and a bit of cadmium yellow medium (deeper than swatch #59).
Deepen	A bit of burnt umber added to the above shadow shade #45.
Lighten	Pale yellow basket shade #50.
Streaks	Permanent green light mixed with a bit of burnt umber (similar to swatch #38).
Tomato	
Undercoat	Cadmium yellow medium mixed with titanium white to match swatch #20.
Shading color	Cadmium red light or Grumbacher red, thinned slightly with turpentine.
Deeper accent	Raw umber or ivory black added to either of above red shades.
Lighten	Cadmium yellow medium, thinned slightly with turpentine.
Stem and leaves	Above green shade #38 mixed with cadmium yellow medium, shaded with titanium white.

Onions

Undercoat	Titanium white.
Stems and deeper shade	Above green shade #38.
Lighter shade	Cadmium yellow medium added to some of the above green shade to match swatch #39.
Roots	More titanium white added to some of above green shade for a very pale green and titanium white.

Cucumber

Undercoat	Above green shade #38.
Lighten	Above green shade #39.

Eggplant

Undercoat	Cobalt violet mixed with raw umber or ivory black with a bit of alizaran crimson added as desired.
Deeper shading	Ivory black, thinned slightly with turpentine.
Lighter shading	Titanium white.
Leaves and stem	Above green shade #38.
Deeper shading	Eggplant shade.
Lighter shading	Pale yellow.

Turnip

Undercoat	Titanium white mixed with a bit of raw umber and cadmium yellow medium (similar to swatch #21).
Deeper shading	Titanium white added to above eggplant color (lighter than swatch #32).
Leaves	Above green shades #38 and #39. Titanium white and eggplant color added for contrast.

Carrots

Undercoat	Cadmium yellow medium mixed with cadmium red light, a bit of burnt sienna, and titanium white (similar to swatch #55).
Deeper shading	Burnt sienna added to some of above color (similar to swatch #57).
Deeper accent	Burnt sienna mixed with titanium white to match #58.
Lighter shading	Titanium white.
Leaves	Permanent green light mixed with viridian green and a bit of burnt sienna (deeper than swatch #34).
Veins	Green-brown shade.

Corn

Undercoat	Cadmium yellow medium, thinned slightly with turpentine.
Accent streaks	Burnt sienna, thinned with turpentine.
Kernels	Cadmium yellow medium mixed with titanium white to match swatch #21.

Husks	Cadmium yellow medium added to green shade #37; raw umber added to green shade #38.
Radishes	
Undercoat	Grumbacher red, thinned slightly with turpentine.
Deeper shading	Grumbacher red mixed with a bit of raw umber, thinned slightly with turpentine.
Lighter shading	Cadmium yellow medium mixed with titanium white to match swatch #21, thinned slightly with turpentine.
Leaves	Yellow or brown added to green shades #38 and #39 as needed.

Lesson Pattern

Basket

Before painting, outline in pen and ink the basket and all the detail of the interlacing slats. This will show through the paint just enough for you to re-accent later with the deeper shading color.

Lift aside a little of the basket shadow shade #49 and add turpentine to it until it is almost water-thin. Bring the thin color over the inside area and around the outlined vegetables. This wash will be dry by the time you start to paint the vegetables.

Clean the brush, fill it with the suggested undercoat color, and paint the entire basket. When this is completed, wipe the brush and fill it with the deeper shade #47. Lightly brush the deeper shade over the upper and lower areas of the basket and at each side. Wipe the brush thoroughly, and use just the wide edge in a back-and-forth motion to lightly blend the edge of these colors together. Wipe the brush when this is completed, and add a little of the off-white (swatch #51). Use this color as a highlight in the basket center and along the upper band, dry-brushing and blending as before. Accent the basket, slats, and upper rim with the deeper shadow shade (swatch #45), using just the tip of the small pointed brush.

Before painting the overlying vegetables, spray with a fixative to quickly dry the basket. Use the fixative after each vegetable is completed before continuing. The squash, tomato, and onion top may be painted while the basket is still moist, but be sure to proceed with caution.

Squash (or Gourd)

Using the large flat brush and the suggested yellow-brown shade, fill in the entire squash, painting just inside the outline. Wipe the brush and add the deeper green-brown to about one-third of the brush width. Lightly brush the deeper color over the outside edge of the squash. Wipe the brush before adding a small amount of the pale yellow to the center area. Wiping the brush frequently, blend these colors together with light whisks of the brush.

Accent the inside center base of the squash with a bit of the lighter shade #45, using the small pointed brush and the thin dark green paint for the detail. Use the same thin dark green paint to apply the irregular streaks down the squash and to accent the deeper color around the stem. Spray with fixative.

Tomato

Use the large flat brush to undercoat the tomato with the yellow shade. Wipe the brush thoroughly. Paint the tomato with Grumbacher red shaded into the deep red. If you would prefer a brighter orange-red, use cadmium red light and deepen only the outside edges with a deeper shade of orange-red. Lift aside a little of the red you are using and add a little raw umber or ivory black to deepen it. Wipe the brush before adding the deeper color to about one-third of the brush width. Keeping the dark to the outside, lightly brush the color around the outside of the tomato. Add more strokes of this color if you wish a darker overall shading. Use the sponge or dry brush to lightly blend the two colors together.

To lighten the center area, use cadmium yellow medium (or a lighter yellow) brushed on and lightly blended with the sponge or a dry brush. Remember to wipe the brush frequently when dry-brushing. Paint the green leaves with the small pointed brush, using the two shades of green. Paint these from the inside, out to a pointed ending. Use spray fixative.

Onions

Since the three small white onions are painted over the shadow color, first paint them with a coat of white. While the white is drying, mix the two green shades. Be sure to prepare enough of the green shade #38 because it will be used to shade nearly all the remaining leaf-green shades. You might want to skip ahead to the cucumber now and drop back to complete the onion shading next.

After you've done the cucumber and the coat of white is dry for the onions, add a few drops of turpentine to a little more white. Paint over the onions with the small flat brush. Use the lighter green and edge with the deeper green. As you first paint the underneath onion stems, be sure to reverse the brush so that the light and dark areas are in contrast. Paint each stem from the outside in toward the white. When the stems are done, wipe the brush and lightly whisk the green into the white onion. Continue the light back-and-forth whisks, blending a little green into the onion and a little white up into the green stem for a streaked and uneven effect.

Use the small pointed brush and thinned paint to paint the uneven onion roots, being sure to contrast the root color against the basket shadow. Finish the ends of the onion stems by accenting the center with a lighter yellow-green and painting a thin circle of dark green around each one. Use spray fixative.

Cucumber

Use the large flat brush to undercoat the cucumber in the deeper green shade #38. Clean this brush and put it aside for later use. Fill only one side of the small flat brush with lighter green paint, keeping this color to the outside while edging the entire cucumber. Wipe the brush to remove any of the dark green undercoat, and again fill only one side of the flat brush with the lighter green. Paint the stripes from top to bottom, beginning at the left or right and adding the center stripe last.

After wiping the brush, use it to blend the colors lightly together around the stem area. If the lighter stripes appear too pronounced, use the flat brush to whisk very lightly over and blend them slightly. Paint the stem with the small pointed brush and dark green paint. Accent the stem end with a bit of pale yellow or white, adding a thin circle of dark green around this and at the base of the stem. Use spray fixative.

Eggplant

Undercoat the eggplant in the deep purple shade with the large flat brush. Wipe the brush before adding a small amount of black to the wide edge of the brush. Lightly streak the black from the base upward, accenting the lower right side more heavily. Wipe the brush thoroughly before edging the tip of the brush in white. Add the white highlights with light strokes from the upper right down into the deeper color. Wipe the brush frequently as the white is blended.

Paint the larger leaves with the large flat brush and the smaller leaves and stem with the tip of the large pointed brush. Paint the large leaves with a thin undercoat of green as you did in the grape lesson. Brush the pale yellow over the green for the lighter side of the leaf. Use the eggplant color to deepen the opposite side, being certain to contrast the lighter side of the upper leaf against the deeper side of the lower leaf. Use the small pointed brush and thin dark paint for the leaf veins. Follow with the spray fixative.

Turnips

Undercoat the turnips with the large flat brush, using the pale cream color. Wipe the brush thoroughly before adding a small amount of the pale violet shade to one half of the brush. Outline the turnip with the shade, adding more color as it is needed. Wipe the brush before adding a very small amount of the deeper eggplant shade to one edge of the brush. Accent the base of the turnip with eight upward streaks of the deeper shade. Add more of the deeper color when necessary. Accent the stem area with light downward streaks of the deeper color, lightly dry-brushing for a soft blending. Add white to the center area if you want a lighter highlight.

Paint the leaves with the small flat brush, using the suggested green shades. Shade the lighter leaves with white and use the deeper eggplant color to shade the deeper edges. Paint the slightly curled leaves from the inside out and contrast the overlapping leaves with an edge of white or deep purple. Spray with fixative.

Carrots

Using the small flat brush and the yellow shade #55 undercoat the carrots. Use the deeper shade #57 to shade the underneath carrot (area J in Pattern #40) more heavily before shading the overlying carrot (area K in Pattern #40). Deepen the lower right side of the carrot (area K) with shade #51, adding a little of shade #58 if necessary. Wipe the brush and lightly blend these colors together.

Add white to the top and left side of carrot (area K), and lightly dry-brush for a slightly lighter effect. Use the small pointed brush to paint the deeper shaded commas over the carrots and to accent the thin tapering roots.

Use the small flat brush and thin green paint on the jagged carrot leaves. Paint these from the inside out, tipping the corner of the brush to end each stroke on a fine point. Paint the leaf veins with the small pointed brush in a deeper shade of green-brown. Spray with fixative.

Corn

Fill the large flat brush with the thinned yellow paint and heavily undercoat the corncob outline. Wipe the brush and add the slightly thinned brown shade to one corner. With the narrow side of the brush, paint three or four lengthwise streaks of brown down the length of the cob.

Clean the brush and put it aside. Paint the kernels next, using the small flat brush and the pale yellow shade. Do not thin this color so that the kernels will remain ridged for a roughly textured effect. Use the square tip of the small brush to paint each vertical row of corn. Press and slide the brush slightly across the ear of corn to form each kernel as you paint down each row. The brush will be picking up some of the deeper yellow and brown for additional shading. Wipe the brush whenever necessary before adding more of the pale yellow.

Using either the large pointed or the large flat brush, paint the husks from the top down, over the sides and into the tapered ends. When using the lighter green, blend white on the brush for a lighter shading. Add a little thin raw umber on the side of the brush with the deeper green for more contrast. Be sure to contrast the light and dark areas of the husks wherever they overlap. Spray corn with fixative.

Radishes

Undercoat the radishes with Grumbacher red, that is slightly thinned with turpentine. Use the small flat brush to paint both the radishes and the leaves. Deepen each side of the radishes with the deeper oxblood shade, wiping the brush frequently as they are dry-brushed for a blended effect. Add the pale yellow to the center area, and dry-brush into the red for a lighter shading.

Use the small flat brush with the deeper green to paint the underneath leaf. Use the lighter green, blended with an edge of white, to paint the upper leaf, adding the veins with the small pointed brush and thin dark green paint.

When the design is completed, scatter a few dewdrops over many of the vegetables for a garden-fresh appearance.

Pattern #40

LESSON 35

Compositions in Gold

Gold oil color will always need to be thinned with drops of turpentine until it is of an easy flowing consistency. It can be used alone or combined on the brush with another color for an infinite variety of attractive effects. In this lesson the gold has been used alone to lighten and highlight some of the areas; it has also been combined with other colors for a subtle shading. You may wish to experiment dry-brushing the thin gold paint over some of your previous lesson sheets. Lesson 17 is a good one to try because the faint shimmer of gold will dramatize the brown and white shades. Gold paint is sold in several forms, but the tube oil—just like the tube oil paints you have been using—provides the best quality and consistency. Use Malfa gold, or you may want to experiment with Malfa silver (both are made by Weber).

Gold may be used alone—or combined with a color—to paint the various borders of scrollwork you may need to complete the finishing detail on many decorative objects. The lesson subject itself can be changed by the addition of gold. For instance, the folk art lesson could be completely changed by using gold in place of the white for shading the designs. The lesson on pine cones and pineapples can easily be varied by dry-brushing the pineapples with thin gold instead of white. The green needles surrounding the pine cones could be shaded with gold for a very attractive holiday effect. And all flowers, soldiers, and federal designs can all be painted with some gold in the shading for a more interesting effect.

Here are three other uses for gold (and you will probably discover many other ways to use this versatile and attractive paint):

Photograph #41

- When decorating clear glass jars or bottles, add a little background color to the glass with the gold paint. Thin the gold and use a small, coarse, bristle brush to apply the paint. The coarse bristles and thin paint will produce an irregular hit-and-miss deposit of gold as the brush is moved around and around the jar. If you wish a heavier gold background, apply the gold a second or third time. When this is dry, paint the design over the gold paint.

- The same coarse brush and thin gold paint can be used to brush lightly the outside areas of painted or antiqued wood panels. This must be used sparingly and is even more effective when a decorative brass ring is used at the top of the panel for accent.
- Gold paint is ideal for antiquing furniture, too. Thin with turpentine, and brush it sparingly over the surface. Blend the gold with a soft cloth for a smooth effect. Here, again, the fingertips can be used to blend lightly. Carved or sculptured furniture that has been painted a light color and antiqued in a darker shade can really be enhanced with a light brushing of gold over the raised portions. After painting this lesson you will surely find other original ways to use gold in your future decorative designs.

As you paint this design, you will be able to decide how much, or how little, gold to use for the effect you prefer. If you use lighter shades of the fruit colors with gold, this design will become delicately shaded. Experiment using the gold paint in place of the white or any other pale color used to lighten fruit.

Brushes

Cornucopia	Large pointed brush
Apple, peach, and leaves	Large flat brush
Grapes	Small flat brush
Curliques and leaf veins	Small pointed brush

Colors

Leaves	Gold oil color, shaded with burnt sienna, thinned with turpentine.
Peach	Cadmium red light mixed with a bit of burnt sienna and a bit of white to match swatch #54.
Apple	Grumbacher red mixed with a bit of raw umber, thinned with turpentine.
Grapes	Cobalt violet mixed with a bit of raw umber to deepen, thinned with turpentine.
Cornucopia	Gold oil color, shaded with burnt sienna, thinned with turpentine.
Deeper shading	Raw umber, thinned with turpentine.
Lighter shading	Gold, thinned with turpentine.
Leaf veins	Raw umber or burnt sienna added to some of the above leaf shade for a dark green. (Burnt sienna also may be used alone for the veins.)

Lesson Pattern

Leaves

When pattern #41 is ready and your paints are mixed, start to paint all the leaves and fruit that will be overlapped by others. Begin with the larger grape leaf and the small half-leaf. The smaller leaves may be painted either now or after the fruit is completed.

Fill half of the flat brush with the green shade before adding the gold on the opposite side of the brush. Keep the green to the outside as you outline the leaves in both colors. (Follow the leaf-painting directions given in Lesson 25.)

With both green and gold on the brush, fill in the entire leaf with curved strokes, beginning at the center and extending outward. Wipe the brush, fill it with gold, and brush additional curved strokes over the leaves, adding more or less gold for the effect that is pleasing to you.

Accenting the edges of gold leaves with a darker color is often necessary so that they will contrast against other areas of gold or color in a design.

Accent the darker edges of the grape leaf with raw umber thinned with a few drops of turpentine. Slide the flat edge of the brush into the brown, picking up only a small amount of this color along the edge. Lightly brush the brown over the leaf edge, painting either from just inside the leaf outward or from the outside edge inward. Since these should be very short, light strokes using only a little paint in the brush, you will need to pick up the brown frequently.

Paint the smaller leaves surrounding the pattern with both gold and green on the brush for a shaded stroke. Use the small pointed brush with thin brown or dark green paint to accent the leaf veins lightly. You may prefer to add the veins after the entire design is completed so that you can vary this color if necessary for a lighter or darker accent. Use the spray fixative now to hasten the drying time of the leaves and again after the peach and apple are painted.

Peach

Paint the peach next, using the suggested red shade. This design can be painted more easily if you turn the pattern whenever necessary. In this case, turn the pattern upside-down to paint the peach from the center top and around each side. Half-fill the large flat brush with the red shade and outline the fruit, leaving

Pattern #41

the center free of color. Clean the brush in turpentine and fill it with the gold paint.

Begin applying the gold in the center area just inside the red shade. Wipe the brush before using very light strokes to smooth and blend the gold slightly into the red. Again, wipe the brush and add the deeper red shade to the lower inside corner of the brush. Lightly paint the deeper-shaded bulge line along the right side of the peach and blend it into the gold paint.

Stop a moment and look at the finished peach. If the effect is pleasing to you, leave it alone. If you would like more red in the fruit, add light strokes of this color over the gold. Since the fruit colors are still wet, re-accenting them with either color or gold for a softly blended effect is easy. Spray with fixative.

Apple

Paint the apple now so that a few grapes can extend over it later on if you choose. Use the deeper red shade in the flat brush to outline the apple in the same manner as the peach. As you paint, remember that you are substituting gold for the lighter shading on each fruit. If you like the effect of more color than gold, bring the color over a wider portion of the fruit before the gold is added, using less gold to lighten and highlight. Spray with fixative.

Grapes

The grapes are most easily painted with the small flat brush. Using only the violet shade in the brush, outline each underneath grape. Wipe the brush and lightly fill it with the gold color. Take one or two short, curved strokes to fill the unpainted area of these grapes. Wipe the brush and lightly blend the two colors of each grape so that you will have no trouble contrasting the dark and light area against other grapes. When the shading of the underneath grapes is completed, paint all the overlapping grapes in the same manner, beginning at the lower part of the cluster and painting upward to the top.

Cornucopia

Add a few drops of turpentine to the gold paint so that it flows easily from the large pointed brush. As you fill the brush with the gold, press firmly so that it is flattened and completely filled with paint. Begin painting the cornucopia from the outside upper flared edge. Paint over the apple and curve into a line under the grapes. Take two or three strokes to fill the wider sections of this pattern. As you paint each section of the cornucopia, leave a hairline separation between each curved row. This will be a guideline to placing the brown shading strokes later. Refill the brush when necessary to produce a flowing stroke.

After the gold is applied, add a few drops of turpentine to a small amount of burnt sienna, using the spatula to mix the thin color. Fill the brush with gold, turn the right side of the brush into the edge of thin burnt sienna, and stroke only once or twice. Keeping the brown on the upper right side of the brush, begin to shade the gold at the upper curve of the cornucopia. Turn the brush so that the brown is at the left, and complete shading the lower top. Add more gold and brown whenever necessary.

To complete the shading, keep the brown on the left side of the brush to cover and connect the hairline separation of the gold undercoat. Using a little burnt sienna on the brush with the gold produces a copper color that you may find a desirable shade for future decorating.

After this design is dry, additional gold or color highlights can still be added if you choose. The brown and gold color combination is also effective when used for borders and scrollwork around a painted design. By experimenting with gold and other colors in varying designs, you will be able to create unique effects.

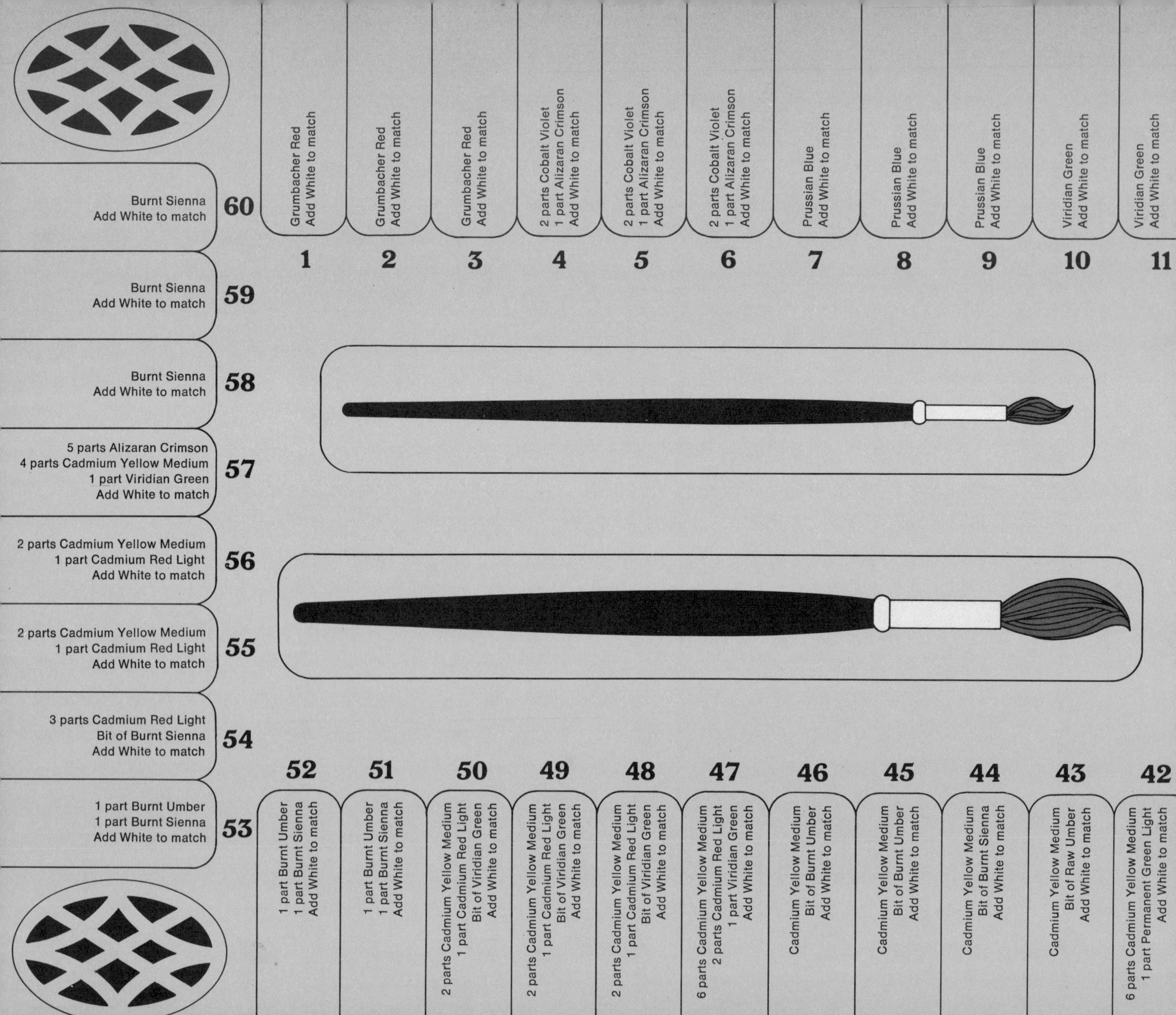
1
Grumbacher Red
Add White to match
2
Grumbacher Red
Add White to match
3
Grumbacher Red
Add White to match
4
2 parts Cobalt Violet
1 part Alizaran Crimson
Add White to match
5
2 parts Cobalt Violet
1 part Alizaran Crimson
Add White to match
6
2 parts Cobalt Violet
1 part Alizaran Crimson
Add White to match
7
Prussian Blue
Add White to match
8
Prussian Blue
Add White to match
9
Prussian Blue
Add White to match
10
Viridian Green
Add White to match
11
Viridian Green
Add White to match
42
6 parts Cadmium Yellow Medium
1 part Permanent Green Light
Add White to match
43
Cadmium Yellow Medium
Bit of Raw Umber
Add White to match
44
Cadmium Yellow Medium
Bit of Burnt Sienna
Add White to match
45
Cadmium Yellow Medium
Bit of Burnt Umber
Add White to match
46
Cadmium Yellow Medium
Bit of Burnt Umber
Add White to match
47
6 parts Cadmium Yellow Medium
2 parts Cadmium Red Light
1 part Viridian Green
Add White to match
48
2 parts Cadmium Yellow Medium
1 part Cadmium Red Light
Bit of Viridian Green
Add White to match
49
2 parts Cadmium Yellow Medium
1 part Cadmium Red Light
Bit of Viridian Green
Add White to match
50
2 parts Cadmium Yellow Medium
1 part Cadmium Red Light
Bit of Viridian Green
Add White to match
51
1 part Burnt Umber
1 part Burnt Sienna
Add White to match
52
1 part Burnt Umber
1 part Burnt Sienna
Add White to match
53
1 part Burnt Umber
1 part Burnt Sienna
Add White to match
54
3 parts Cadmium Red Light
Bit of Burnt Sienna
Add White to match
55
2 parts Cadmium Yellow Medium
1 part Cadmium Red Light
Add White to match
56
2 parts Cadmium Yellow Medium
1 part Cadmium Red Light
Add White to match
57
5 parts Alizaran Crimson
4 parts Cadmium Yellow Medium
1 part Viridian Green
Add White to match
58
Burnt Sienna
Add White to match
59
Burnt Sienna
Add White to match
60
Burnt Sienna
Add White to match